THE DIVINE COMEDY
Volume I

DANTE ALIGHIERI
THE DIVINE COMEDY

translated by Thomas G. Bergin
&
illustrated by Leonard Baskin

GROSSMAN PUBLISHERS
NEW YORK 1969

Illustrations Copyright © 1969 by Leonard Baskin
Text Copyright in all countries of the International Copyright Union
All rights reserved
Library of Congress catalogue card number 70-86117
Published by Grossman Publishers, Inc.
125A East 19th Street, New York 10003
Published simultaneously in Canada by Fitzhenry and Whiteside Ltd.
Text printed in Italy
Illustrations printed in the United States of America
Bound in the United States of America
First Printing

TRANSLATOR'S NOTE

The present translation was originally prepared for the Crofts Classics; the version of the Inferno appeared in that series in 1948, the Purgatory in 1953 and the Paradise in 1954. In 1955 the three parts were published together in one volume, The Divine Comedy. I should like to thank the publishers, Appleton-Century-Crofts, for allowing me to make use of the version of the Crofts Classics in the preparation of this new one. The principal difference, in fact, between this translation and that of the Crofts Classics is that I have here translated in full the passages that were summarized in the earlier edition; I have also revised a number of lines.

I should like to record here my gratitude to the late Dr. Gilbert E. Cunningham of Alva, Scotland, both for his sympathetic understanding of my approach and for his excellent suggestions for improving certain lines and passages.

I append a list of authorities referred to in the Notes, omitting those for whom full information is provided in the appropriate individual Note.

T. G. B.

Madison, Connecticut
    June, 1969

★

ANDREOLI: La Divina Commedia di Dante Alighieri col commento di Raffaello Andreoli. Firenze: 1891.

ANONIMO: Commento alla Divina Commedia di Anonimo fiorentino del secolo XV ora per la prima volta stampata a cura di Pietro Fanfani. Bologna: 1866-74.

BENVENUTO: Benvenuti de Rambaldis de Imola Comentum super Dantis Aldigherij comoediam nunc primum integre in lucem editum sumptibus Guilielmi Warren Vernon curante Jacobo Philippo Lacaita. Florentiae: 1887.

BOCCACCIO: Esposizione sopra la Comedia di Dante, a cura di G. Padoan. Milano: 1965.

BUTI: Commento di Francesco da Buti sopra la Divina Commedia di Dante Alighieri pubblicato per cura di Crescentino Giannini. Pisa: 1858-62.

CASINI-BARBI: Dante Alighieri. La Divina Commedia col commento di Tommaso Casini a cura di S. A. Barbi. Firenze: 1952.

CHIMENZ: La Divina Commedia di Dante Alighieri a cura di Siro A. Chimenz. Torino: 1963.

COMPAGNI: Dino Compagni, Chronicle, translated by Else C. M. Benecke and A. G. Ferrers Howell. London: 1906.

DEL LUNGO: La Divina Commedia commentata da Isidoro Del Lungo. Firenze: 1926.

FLAMINI: F. Flamini, Introduction to the Study of the Divine Comedy. Boston: 1910.

FLETCHER: J. B. Fletcher, Symbolism of the Divine Comedy. New York: 1921.

FRATICELLI: La Divina Commedia di Dante Alighieri col commento di Pietro Fraticelli (nuova ed.). Firenze: 1892.

GMELIN: Die Göttliche Komödie übersetzt von Hermann Gmelin; Kommentar. Stuttgart: 1954-7.

MAZZONI: Guido Mazzoni, Almae Luces Malae Cruces. Bologna: 1941.

MOMIGLIANO: Attilio Momigliano, La Divina Commedia. Firenze: 1948.

MOORE: Edward Moore, Studies in Dante, First Series. Oxford: 1896.

NARDI: Bruno Nardi, Saggi di filosofia dantesca (2ª ed. accresciuta). Firenze: 1967.

OTTIMO: L'Ottimo Commento della Divina Commedia, testo inedito d'un contemporaneo di Dante. Pisa: 1827.

PARODI: E. G. Parodi, «La costruzione e l'ordinamento del paradiso dantesco» in Studi letterari e linguistici dedicati a Pio Rajna. Firenze: 1911.

PORENA: La Divina Commedia di Dante Alighieri commentata da Manfredi Porena (nuova ed.). Bologna: 1965.

SAPEGNO: La Divina Commedia a cura di Natalino Sapegno. Firenze: 1955-7.

SAYERS: Dorothy Sayers, Introductory Papers on Dante. New York: 1954.

SCARTAZZINI: Dante Alighieri – La Divina Commedia col commento scartazziniano rifatto da Giuseppe Vandelli. Milano: 1952.

TORRACA: Divina Commedia nuovamente commentata da F. Torraca. Roma-Napoli: 1933.

TOYNBEE: Paget Toynbee, A Dictionary of Proper Names and Notable Matters in the Works of Dante. Oxford: 1898.

VILLANI: Selections from the First Nine Books of the Croniche Fiorentine of Giovanni Villani, translated by Rose E. Selfe, edited by Philip H. Wicksteed. Westminster: 1897.

VOSSLER: Karl Vossler, Mediaeval Culture (reprint). New York: 1958.

INFERNO

CANTO I

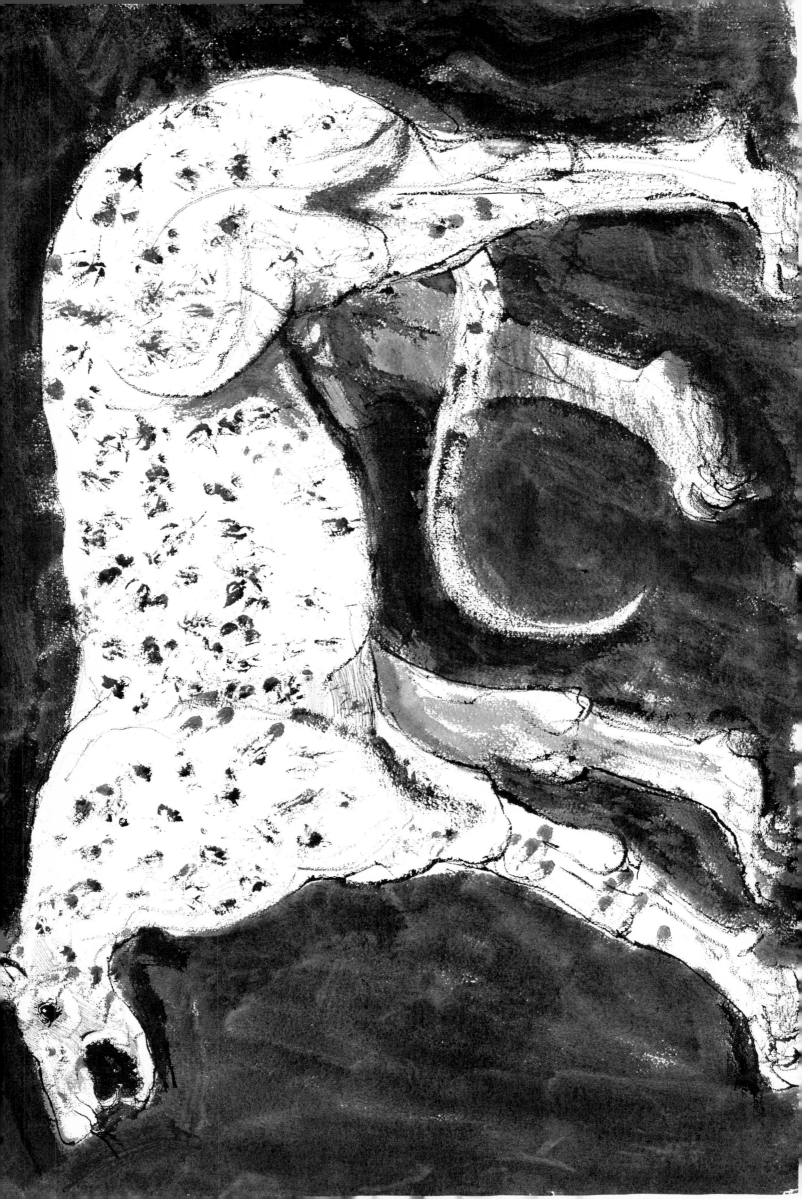

And lo! there then appeared at the hill's base
A lightsome Leopard, nimbly quick and all
Bespotted with a multi-colored pelt.

Inferno I, 30–32

Midway along the journey of our life
I found myself within a gloomy wood
For the right pathway had been lost to view.
So hard it is its aspect to define,
This savage, harsh, and fearsome wilderness,   5
That fear rekindles with the memory.
Bitter it is, yea, death is scarcely more,
Yet to recall the good I found in it
I'll speak too of the other things I saw.

I cannot truly tell how I came there,   10
For, as we walk unknowing in a dream,
So witless had I wandered from the road.
But when at length I stood beneath a hill
That closed the vale so dreadful to my heart
I looked on high and saw its slopes aglow   15
With the rising rays of that consoling star
Whose light leads one aright on every path.
Then did I somewhat still within my heart
The fear that filled me through that anxious night,
And, like to one who, drawing weary breath,   20
Comes from the ocean safe at last to shore
And turns to scan the watery dangers passed,
So did my tremulous soul, still fugitive,
Turn back to gaze again upon that tract
Wherein no soul has ever stayed – and lived.   25

After I had somewhat with rest renewed
My weary body, I took up again
My way upon the desert shore, so shaped
That always firmer fixed was the lower foot.
And lo! there then appeared at the hill's base   30
A lightsome Leopard, nimbly quick and all

3

Bespotted with a multi-colored pelt,
Nor would the beast turn off and let me pass
But rather so impeded my advance
That more than once I turned as to return.   35

The hour was early morn, the rising sun
Climbed in the company of those same stars
That were his escort when in dawn of life
God's love gave motion to these creatures fair.
So that the time and smiling season both   40
Gave me good cause for hope 'gainst that wild thing
Of brilliant hue, yet not so much that I
Could bear unfrightened the successive sight.
For next a Lion, seeming bent to spring,
Emerged, head high and ravening in his rage   45
So that it seemed he filled the air with dread.
Last came a She-Wolf forth, her gauntness charged
With gnawing avarice, for she indeed
Has made life lean for many folk before.
In fear of her and of her aspect fierce   50
I lost the new born hope of the ascent,
And even as one who happy in his gain
Sees that hour come when he must lose it all
And weeps and grows all heavy in his heart,
So I became before that restless beast   55
Who ever drawing nearer drove me back
Down the decline where the sun's rays were stilled.

As I fell back, retreating down the slope,
One stood before my eyes whose voice it seemed
Long silence had enfeebled. When I saw   60
That figure in the wilderness so vast
I cried out to him, "Shade or living man,

Last came a She-Wolf forth, her gauntness charged
With gnawing avarice.

Inferno I, 47–48

Whate'er you be, have pity on my plight."
He answered, "Living man no more, though once
I was, and born of Lombard strain for both   65
My parents were of Mantua; my birth
Came late in time of Julius and I lived
In good Augustus' reign in pagan Rome
When false and lying gods were still adored.
Poet I was and sang of that good son   70
Of old Anchises, fugitive from Troy
After proud Ilion had been razed by flames.
But you, why slip you back to misery?
Why not ascend the fair and smiling mount,
The source and origin of all man's joy!"   75

"Are you then Virgil, spring of poesy,
Fountain of eloquence and golden speech?"
I answered him in timid reverence.
"Honor and light of other bards, I pray,
Bestead me now the zeal and the great love   80
That made me study to seek out your works;
You are my master, my authority,
And you alone the one from whom I drew
The fair style that has won renown for me.
See now this beast for whom I turned my steps,   85
And give me aid against her, famous sage,
For sight of her has chilled my very veins."

To me in tears he answered, "If you would
Seek to find refuge from this savage strand,
Another path must offer you escape,   90
For this foul beast of whom you make complaint
Lets none pass by, nay rather does to death
Such as she meets; so cruel and fell she is

5

That never glutted are her thirsty jaws,
For hunger waxes as her belly fills.   95
Many the animals with whom she mates
And more there 'll be before the Greyhound comes
To deal her painful death. His food will be
Nor land nor pelf but wisdom, love and virtue;
Between two Feltros he will have his birth   100
And be the savior of sweet Italy
For whom the maid Camilla gave her life
With Nisus, Turnus, and Euryalus.
From town to town he will drive back the wolf
Till he has forced her back to Hell from whence   105
Envy first loosed her. For your present weal
My counsel is that you should follow me.
I'll guide you hence through an eternal realm
Where you will hear the outcries of despair
And see the long dead spirits in their woe   110
As they bewail each one his second death.
Then shall you meet those happy souls content,
Though burning, in their hope to reach at last,
When it may be, the nation of the blest.
And if it shall be your desire to rise   115
To that fair realm, a soul more fit than I
Will take you in her charge before we part.
For the Imperial Majesty thereof
Does not approve my presence in his court
Because I was a rebel to his law.   120
His Empire knows no frontier but on high
His Kingdom's seat and Holy City stand;
Happy the soul he chooses there to dwell."

Then I replied, "O Poet, I implore,
By that same God whom you did never know,   125

6

If you would save me from these woes and worse,
Your guidance on the road of which you speak
So that my eyes may see Saint Peter's gate
As well as that sad folk your tale describes."

He started off then and I followed after.   130

CANTO II

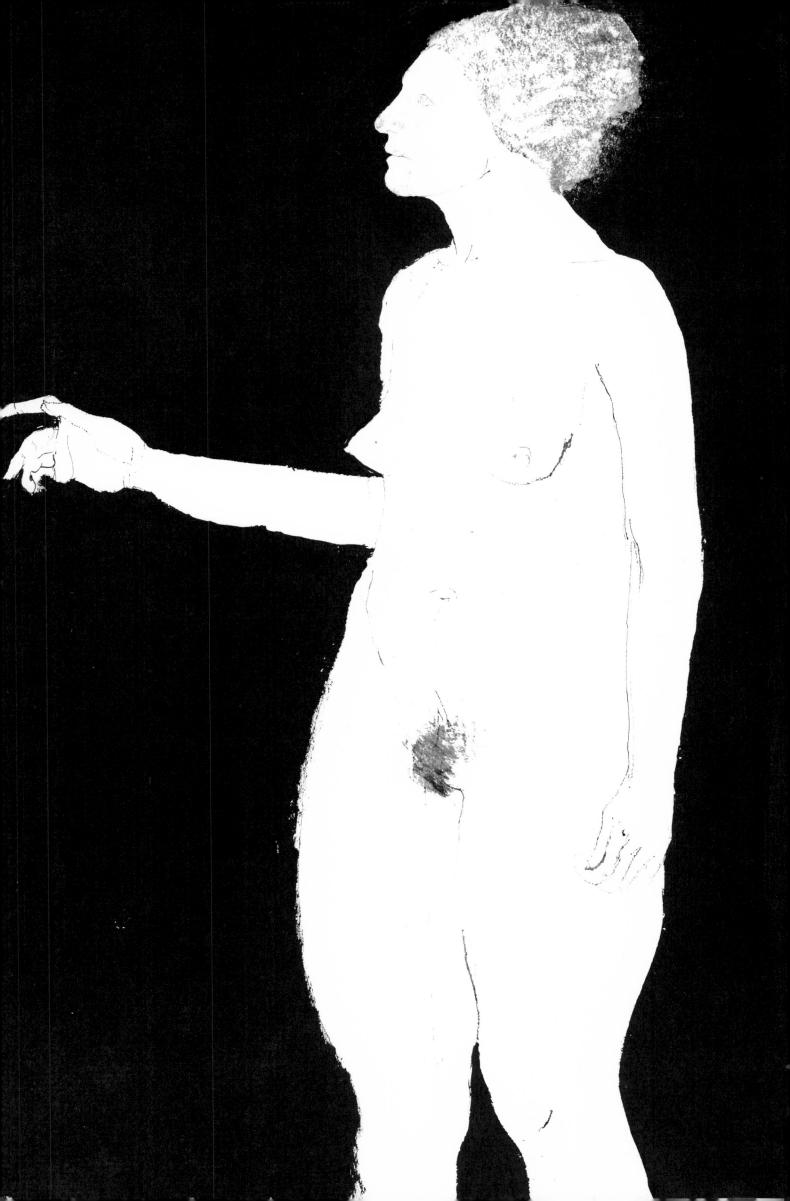

A fair and blessed lady. *Inferno* II, 51

The day was dying and the darkling sky
Was summoning to rest all living things
On earth, save me alone who needs must steel
Myself against the anguish of the road
Before me and my heart against its sights   5
Which memory here will faithfully set forth.

O Muses, O my genius, help me now!
O memory attentive to my course,
Here will appear the measure of your worth.
"Sweet bard who are my guide," thus I began,   10
"Before you lead me on our fearful path
Consider if my virtue may avail.
From your own song I know how Silvio's sire
While yet corruptible did make his way
With human sense intact beyond man's world.   15
Yet if the Adversary of all Ill
Used him thus kindly, not unjust it seems
To men of understanding, for the grace
Of highest wisdom marked him as the sire
Of mother Rome and her Empire to come,   20
Wherein, for so her glory did ordain,
Great Peter's followers should have their seat.
This privileged journey, as your verses vaunt,
Did school him well and so prepare the way
For his great victory and the papal cloak.   25
Of old the chosen vessel of God's grace
Likewise was so translated that he might
Bring heavenly comfort to our new born faith
Which is the gateway to salvation's road.
But who am I such privilege to receive?   30
Aeneas am I not, nor am I Paul,
And I and others scarce would think me fit

For such a venture. If I follow you
I fear the folly of so bold a course.
You know my thoughts, O Sage, beneath my words." 35

And thus as one undoing his resolve
And changing purpose with a second thought
So that his mind swerves from his first fixed aim,
Such was my mood on that benighted slope;
I stood to wreck by thought the enterprise 40
My former resolution had embraced.

"If I have understood your words aright,"
The shade of that great spirit answered me,
"Your soul is stricken by weak cowardice
Which often turns us back from honor's goal 45
As fancied dangers turn a shying horse.
Now that this fear may loose you from its grip
I'll tell you why I came and what I heard
When first my heart was stirred to grief for you.
I was with those suspended when there came 50
To summon me a fair and blessed lady,
Such that I begged her only to command me.
Her eyes were luminous as Love's own star
And with angelic accents in her voice
She thus began her discourse clear and sweet: 55
'O courtly soul of Mantua, whose fame
Still lives on earth and shall while earth shall last,
My friend – and Fortune's foe – is sore beset
Upon a lonely heath. Dismayed he turns
From his true path. Report of him on high 60
Is such I fear my aid may come too late.
Do you now with your golden counsel go
And with all other succor he may need,

12

And bring him comfort and console my tears.
'Tis Beatrice who speeds you on your way;   65
I come from whence I fain would soon repair;
Love called me forth and Love inspires my speech.
When once again I stand before my Lord
I'll sing your praises to him.' Thus she spoke
And I made answer: 'Lady of such grace   70
By which alone the race of men surpasses
All that is bound within the smallest sphere,
So welcome to my ear is your command
That had I now obeyed it were too late.
No further need you show me your desire;   75
Tell me but this: why do you take no heed
Of thus descending low to this abyss
From Heaven where you long to be again?'
'Since your demand probes deeply,' she replied,
'I'll briefly tell you why no fear prevents   80
My entrance here. Such things alone we fear
As have the power to harm us, but all else
Inspires no fright. I am, by grace of God,
So shaped that misery of this lower world
Touches me not, nor do I feel your flames.   85
A Lady dwells above, whose heart is touched
By his sad plight whom I would have you help,
And her compassion melts harsh laws of Heaven.
She called Lucía and admonished her:
"Now has your faithful liegeman need of you,   90
And to you I commend him." Then Lucía,
The enemy of cruelty, arose
And came where I shared holy Rachel's throne
And spoke: "O Beatrice, true praise of God,
Withhold not help from one who loved you so   95
That for your sake he rose above the herd.

13

Do you not hear his piteous complaint?
Do you not see death peril fronting him
Beside that stream more fearsome than the sea?"
Never was any living thing so quick   100
To seek its own advantage or evade
Its injury than I in coming here
On this reproach. I left my heavenly chair
And put my trust in your just eloquence
That honors you and all who hear you speak.'   105

Her reasons thus revealed she turned aside,
Her glowing eyes bedewed with gentle tears,
And made me with her glance more quick to move.
Thus in fulfillment of her will I came
To you and saved you from that threatening beast   110
That checked you on your path on the hill side.
Why then this hesitation and this pause?
And whence this shameful shrinking in your heart?
And why should courage now abandon you?
Three ladies blessed in the court above   115
Have care for you, and what I have set forth
Is all a pledge and promise of your weal."

Just as a bed of flowers, bent and shrunk
By nighttime chill, when once touched by the sun
Arise and show their petals to his rays,   120
So rose again my courage in my soul
And so much zeal awakened in my heart
That I spoke thus, in spirit free of fear:
"Blessed be she whose tender heart was moved
To succor me, and blessed your swift heed   125
And courteous obedience to her words.
So has your speech renewed my heart's desire

14

RACHEL

Rachel

LVCIA.

St. Lucía and Rachel.   *Inferno* II, 91 ff.

To undertake the journey, that once more
My former resolution is affirmed.
Lead on, since one sole will now moves us both,   130
Be now my guide and lord and master." Thus
I spoke out boldly, and upon his steps
I followed in the hard and rugged path.

CANTO III

"Through me ye enter in the town of woe,
Through me ye pass into eternal sorrow,
Through me ye join the nation of the lost.
Justice my lofty architect did move
To my creation. Mighty Power Divine,   5
Supremest Wisdom, and Primaeval Love
Established me. Before me there were none
Save timeless things, and timeless I shall stand;
Bid hope farewell, all ye who enter here."

Such words in sombre characters I saw   10
Above a gateway carved and I cried out:
"O master, harsh the warning reads to me."
And he replied, as knowing my concern:
"Here must all frailty be put aside,
And here all craven weakness be forgot;   15
The country I described we enter now
Where you will see the grief-afflicted folk
Forever blinded to the sight of God."

Thus speaking he put forth his hand to mine
With brow serene and then, so comforted,   20
He led me down into the hidden world.
Here sighs and dire laments and cries of woe
Re-echoed through the dark and starless air
So that my eyes were moved to ready tears.
Voices of blasphemy in every tongue,   25
And cries of suffering, outbursts of wrath,
In accents shrill or sunk in deep despair,
Like grains of sand churned in a wind to storm,
Mingled in roaring chorus never still
In that forever cheerless atmosphere.   30

19

"Master," I asked, my brow with horror girt,
"What mean these fearful sounds and who are these
Whom grief so sorely presses?" He replied,
"This hapless style becomes those sorry souls
Whose mortal life earned neither praise nor blame;   35
Here are they mingled with that wicked choir
Of angels who rebelled not against God
Nor yet kept faith with Him but stood apart.
Outcast from Heaven lest they its beauty stain
They yet are barred from dwelling low in Hell,   40
Else might the damned some glory claim of them."
"Master," I asked again, "what is their woe
Constraining them to piteous lament?"
"Let few words here suffice," he answered me,
"These luckless ones are without hope of death   45
And their blind living is of such base sort
That envy fills them for all others' lot.
The world lets no report of them endure,
Pity and justice both hold them in scorn:
We'll speak no more of them; glance and pass on."   50

I looked and saw a banner borne aloft,
Always in restless motion so bestirred
As if despising respite in its course,
And after it came running such a long
Parade of souls that I would ne'er have thought   55
Death had undone so vast a multitude.
So eying them some did I recognize,
And saw and knew again the shade of him
Who cravenly the great refusal made.
Then beyond doubt I knew with certainty   60
This was the party of those shabby souls
Contemptible to God and to his foes.

20

Bearing an ancient oarsman bearded white
Who roared in wrath.

Inferno III, 81-82

These miserable things who never lived
Were here all naked, suffering ceaseless stings
From wasps and dragonflies that swarmed about.   65
Their cheeks were running blood which, mixed with tears
Streamed to the ground, a food for filthy worms.

Turning my glance beyond them I espied
A river shore, thick lined with thronging souls,
And asked: "Allow me, master, here to learn   70
Who stands there yonder and what urge creates
Their eager haste to pass beyond the stream,
As in this darkness dimly I detect."
"This you will know," thus did he make reply,
"When we, as we soon shall, our footsteps fix   75
Upon the dolorous shore of Acheron."
Then, fearing my request were indiscreet,
I bent my eyes and held them low in shame
And said no more until we reached the bank.

As we arrived, behold a bark appeared   80
Bearing an ancient oarsman bearded white
Who roared in wrath: "Woe to you, wicked souls,
Never hope more to see the sun again.
I come to take you to the farther shore
Into eternal gloom and fire and ice.   85
And you, O living creature standing there,
Take leave now of this company of the dead."
But when he saw that I did not obey,
"Not by this path," he said, "nor through such gates
Will you come into port; another bark   90
Lighter than mine awaits your journeying."
My leader answered: "Charon, cease to rage;
These things are willed where will and power are one.

21

Obey and ask no more." Subsiding then
The boatman of that dark and sullen stream   95
Whose eyes were socketed in wheels of flame
No longer stirred his hairy jowls in speech.

But as for those dejected naked souls,
With pallid hue and chattering teeth in fear
They heard the pitiless words addressed to them,   100
And fell to cursing God and their own sires,
The human family, and the time and place
And seed of their conception, and their birth.
Then in a mass they all betook themselves
With woeful wailing toward the fatal brink   105
Awaiting every man who fears not God.
Charon the fiend, his glowing eyes like coals,
Calling them out, gathers them all to him,
Belaboring the laggards with his oar.

And just as leaves swayed by the autumn winds   110
Drop from the tree, each falling in its turn
Until the branch is all despoiled and bare,
So here did Adam's evil seed descend,
And one by one they stepped off from the shore,
Like hawk to hunter's call, at Charon's sign.   115
Thus speed they on their way o'er the dark wave
And scarcely have they left the bank behind
When yet another throng takes up its stand.

"My son," my gracious master here began,
"All souls, whatever be their land or tribe,   120
Who die in wrath of God foregather here,
And prompt they are to cross the dreaded flood,
For spur of God's own justice drives them on

22

So that their fear is changed into desire.
No soul of virtue ever comes this way, 125
Wherefor if Charon made complaint of you,
You may divine the import of his words."

He ceased. And all at once the dreadful land
Gave such a trembling shudder that the fear
Still shakes my mind with its remembered shock. 130
The fissured earth split wide and gave forth wind
And such a flash of crimson lightning flared
That my stunned senses were all overwhelmed
And down I dropped like one whom sleep has seized.

CANTO IV

A heavy thunderclap broke on my brain
And roused me and I came to with a start,
As one in violence awaked from sleep.
Upright I stood and cast my glance about,
Looking with fixed attention through the gloom   5
To learn the nature of the place. In truth
I found myself upon the outer rim
Which crowns the valley of the dismal pit
Resounding with interminable laments.
So deep and dim and nebulous it was   10
That though I strove to pierce it with my gaze
I might discern no clear outlines below.

"Now we go down into the lightless world,"
The poet thus began, all pale in hue,
"I shall be first and you will be the second."   15
And I, observant of his pallor, asked,
"How shall I dare to come if you feel fear,
Who are the wonted comfort of my doubts?"
He answered: "It is anguish for the souls
Down here that on my countenance depicts   20
The pity that your eye mistakes for fear.
Now let us onward, for the way is long."
Thus he set forth and thus he led me in
To the first circle girding the abyss.

Herein so far as I could judge by ear   25
No lamentations were there – only sighs
Which moved to trembling the timeless air.
Such was the way of sorrow without pain
That marked the great and thronging multitude
Of infants, women, and the men of old   30
Here dwelling. "Do you not" – the master spoke –

"Inquire now what spirits can these be?
Before proceeding further you must know
These souls are sinless but their merits fail
To save them, for baptism they never had   35
Which is the portal to your rightful faith.
And since before Christ's day their lives were spent
They might not dutifully adore their God,
And of their number I myself am one.
For such defect and for no other crime   40
We are forlorn and suffer only this:
That without hope we live on in desire."

Hearing his words great grief seized on my heart,
For well I knew that many noble souls
Dwelt in that Limbo without hope or fear.   45
"Pray tell me now, my master and my lord,"
Thus I began, seeking that certainty
Of firm conviction beyond fear of doubt,
"Did any yet go hence to blessedness
By merit of his own or of another?"   50
And he, who understood my covert speech,
Replied, "I was but recent in this state,
When here below a Mighty One descended,
Crowned with the sign of victory on his brow.
He drew from us our primal father's shade,   55
And his son Abel, and the shade of Noah,
And faithful Moses, bringer of the Law,
And Father Abraham, David the King,
And Israel with his father and his sons,
And Rachel for whose sake he toiled so long.   60
These and full more he raised among the blessed.
Before these spirits, I would have you learn,
No human soul salvation had achieved."

And of their number I myself am one.
For such defect and for no other crime
We are forlorn and suffer only this:
That without hope we live on in desire.

Inferno IV, 39–42

While thus he talked we did not slow our pace,
But moved on through the press of ancient shades   65
As thick around us as trees in a wood.
Our way had taken us not very far
From my awakening when I saw a glow
Prevailing o'er a hemisphere of shadow.
We were as yet some way removed from it   70
But not so much that I could not discern
That honorable folk possessed that place.
"O ornament of wisdom and of art,
Tell me," I asked, "what glory sets apart
These that bide here from the surrounding gloom?"   75
And he made answer: "Glorious report
They left behind them in your world above
This meed of heavenly favor wins for them."
At this a voice broke in upon my ear,
"All honor to the loftiest of bards,   80
His shade that left us, lo, it now returns."
And as the words ceased, I saw four great souls
Approaching us, their aspect neither gay
Nor melancholy. My good master spoke:
"Mark you the one who strides before the rest,   85
As if their captain, bearing sword in hand?
Homer is he, the poet sovereign.
Horace the satirist comes on his heels,
The third is Ovid, Lucan follows last.
Since all may share with me the name one spoke,   90
They honor me and therein they do well."
Thus did my eyes behold the blessed school
United round the lord of song sublime,
Which eagle-like soars high above its mates.
When they had parleyed for a while together   95
They turned to me with mien benevolent

Which my lord witnessed with a gracious smile.
And greater honor still they granted me,
Admitting me to join their fellowship,
So I was sixth in that academy.   100

Then towards the radiance we bent our steps,
Speaking the while of what was proper there,
But here would hardly profit to repeat.
Under a noble castle then we stood
Which high walls sevenfold did gird about,   105
In turn enveloped by a flowing stream.
O'er this we passed as though it were dry land,
And through seven portals by these sages led
I came unto a meadow fresh and green.
Therein I found a people grave of glance,   110
Having the aspect of authority,
Speaking few words in low and subdued tones.
We took our stand apart, upon a rise
Whose open prominence allowed our gaze
Full prospect of this virtuous family.   115
Thus from that verdant vantage point the great
And glorious spirits past were shown to me
Whose names with exultation I recall.

I saw Electra with many standing near,
Among whom Hector I could recognize,   120
Aeneas too and hawk-eyed Caesar armed,
I saw Camilla and Penthesilea
On the other side; I saw too King Latinus
Sitting beside Lavinia, his daughter;
I saw the Brutus who drove Tarquin forth,   125
Lucretia, Julia, Marcia and Cornelia,
And Saladin, standing alone, apart.

30

And when I raised my lids a little higher
I saw the master of all those that know
Sitting among his philosophic family. 130
All look to him, all pay him reverence;
There I beheld Plato and Socrates
Who closer than the rest stand at his feet,
Democritus who builds the world on chance,
Diogenes and Thales, Anaxagoras, 135
Empedocles, Zeno and Heraclitus;
I marked that harvester of qualities,
Dioscorides I mean, and Orpheus too,
Tully and Linus, Seneca moralist,
Euclid geometrist and Ptolemy, 140
Hippocrates, Avicenna, Galen, and
Averroes who wrote the great comment.
I cannot fully speak of all of them:
My lengthy theme so presses me that often
The tale falls short in telling of the deed. 145
The company of six divides in two;
My sage guide leads me on another path,
Out of the quiet, into the quivering air
And soon I come to where no light is seen.

CANTO V

So downward to the second ring we moved,
Whose smaller scope encloses greater woe,
Driving its prisoners to dreadful groans.
There stands the snarling Minos, fearful judge,
And probes the sins of all who enter in,   5
And gives his verdict with his coiling tail.
Thus is his usage: when the luckless soul
Comes to his presence it confesses all
And that fierce jurist, schooled full well in sin,
Considers the most fitting sphere of Hell,   10
And thereon wraps his tail about himself
With coils whose numbers match the zone assigned.
The sinners ever press, before his bar
And each in turn steps forth to learn his doom;
They speak, their sentence hear, and downward fall.   15

"O ye, who come to sorrow's sanctuary,"
Cried Minos, when his eye caught sight of me,
Laying aside the business of his charge,
"Ware how you enter here and whom you trust;
Be not deceived because the way is wide   20
And entrance easy." "Why this vain reproof?"
My master answered, "Seek not to impede
His fated progress, for these things are willed
Where will and power are one. Obey, and ask
No more."

                    And now the swelling notes of woe   25
Become perceptible, now am I come
Where lamentations press upon my ears.
As the wide ocean moans when stormy winds
In mighty conflict lash its watery waste,
So in this circle without ray of light   30

A wind infernal howls without surcease,
And on the wings of the undying gale
The hapless souls are tossed and buffeted.
When they are carried past the ancient cleft
There do they give free rein to sobs and wails   35
And fearfully blaspheme divinity.

This is the state, I learned, to which condemned
Are carnal sinners who subordinate
The rule of reason to their appetites.
And as in winter sky the starlings spread   40
Their wings in wheeling flocks, so here the breath
Of Hell's tornado drives these sorry souls;
Now here, now there, now up, now down they fly,
With never any hope to comfort them
Nor of repose nor of less frenzied flight.   45
As cranes come keening their lugubrious chant,
Trailing in lengthy files across the sky,
So I beheld the shades borne by the wind
Approach us, wailing for their dismal fate.
"Master," I asked, "what souls are these so whipped   50
Through this dark air?" "The first," he told me then,
Was Empress over many tongues; lust-ridden,
To justify her own excesses, she
Made laws to legalize libidinous pleasures.
Semiramis is she, of whom we read   55
That she was wife to Ninus and his heir,
Governing the state that now the Sultan holds.
Next comes the shade of her who for love's sake
Herself did slay and to Sichaeus' ash
Was faithless. Then comes Cleopatra, lewd   60
And lustful queen. Mark Helen there, for whom
So long a term of wasteful war was waged.

And thereon wraps his tail about himself
With coils whose numbers match the zone assigned.

Inferno v, 11–12

See there Achilles peerless, whom at last
"Love overthrew. See Tristam, Paris"; and
A thousand more he pointed out and named,   65
Who for excess of love their lives laid down.

When I had heard my master call the roll
Of ladies fair and noble knights of old,
Pity swept o'er me, and my senses swam.
Then did I speak: "Fain would I word exchange   70
With those two borne together by the wind,
Seeming so light and fragile 'gainst its force."
"When they sweep nearer to us," he replied,
"Ask of them what you will in their love's name
That brought them here, and they will come and speak."   75
And as they wafted toward us on the gale
I raised my voice and cried: "O storm-tossed souls,
Approach and parley if no law forbid."
As turtledoves on wings of soft desire,
With outspread plumes and firm, turn to the nest   80
When love's compulsion homeward summons them,
So came these forth from Dido's numerous train,
Swooping toward us through that malignant air,
Respondent to the warmth of my address.
"O living soul, compassionate and kind,   85
Coming through the dark air to look on us,
Who left a stain of crimson in the world;
If the great Lord of all were but our friend
We should make prayer to him for your peace
Since you have pity for our perverse ill.   90
If there be aught you'd care to say or hear
We shall as readily attend or speak
What time the wind is stilled, as it is now.
The town where I was born stands on the coast

Near where the Po, with his attendant streams   95
Seeking for rest, descends into the sea.
Love which lays sudden hold on gentle hearts
Seized him for my fair body, torn from me
In such a fashion as to grieve me yet.
Love, which absolves no heart beloved from loving,   100
Seized me so strongly for the joy of him
That I am still its captive as you see.
Love led us both together to one death.
Caina waits for him who quenched our lives."
Such were the words that reached us, borne from them.   105

Hearing the tale of these tormented souls
I bowed my head and long I stood downcast
Until the poet asked: "What think you now?"
And when I answered him, "Alas," I said,
"What yearning fancies and what fond desire   110
This loving couple must have led to sin."
And turning then, "Francesca," I began,
"Your suffering calls forth compassion's tears;
But tell me, in the time of love's sweet sighs,
What stratagem of passion urged you on,   115
And wakened guilty yearning in your heart?"
She answered me: "There is no greater pain
Than memory of happy times gone by
In wretchedness – and this your teacher knows.
But if you have such eagerness to learn   120
The first roots of our love, I'll do as one
Who tells a story, weeping as he speaks.
One day, it chanced, for pleasure, we were reading
Of Launcelot and how love bound him fast;
We were alone, of all suspicion free.   125
That reading more than once compelled our eyes

A wind infernal howls without surcease,
And on the wings of the undying gale
The hapless souls are tossed and buffeted.

Inferno v, 31–33

To meet and caused our faces to change color,
But it was one point only that undid us:
When we read how one deeply cherished smile
Was kissed by such a lover – it was then   130
That this soul, who shall never leave my side,
All trembling kissed me full upon the lips . . .
A Gallehaut was the book and he who wrote it
And in it we no further read that day."

While thus one spirit poured her sorrow forth   135
The other wept beside her. Overcome
With pity of the pair I swooned away,
And dropped down lifeless as if death had struck.

CANTO VI

The dragon Cerberus, perceiving us,
Opened his triple jaws and showed his teeth.

Inferno VI, 21–22

As sense comes back to me that fled away
In contemplation of the luckless lot
Of the two kinsmen, moving me to grief,
New torments and new sufferers I see
Where'er I turn, where'er I shift my gaze.   5
This is the third ring, where the rain beats down,
A heavy rain of grim unending chill,
Ever the same its nature and its pulse:
Thick hailstones, water stained, and chilling snow
Through dismal air descend precipitate   10
Upon the soaked and stinking mud beneath.
Here monstrous Cerberus, a savage beast,
With three-fold gullet stands and cur-like howls
Over the folk deep sunken in the slime.
Flame-red eyes and black his slobbering beard,   15
Swollen his paunch, and with his pointed claws
He scratches, strips, and flays the helpless souls.

Under the hail the wretches too give forth
With dog-like howls, writhing about the while
In vain attempts to shield alternate flanks.   20
The dragon Cerberus, perceiving us,
Opened his triple jaws and showed his teeth,
Quivering in every limb with hungry rage.
Whereat my lord did but extend his hand,
Seizing a lump of earth which then he tossed   25
Into the greedy gullet of the beast.
And as the hound that barks to have his meat
But having it his fury then abates,
With chewing of his bone his sole concern,
So did three-snouted Cerberus, whose baying   30
Incessant make the dead wish they were deaf.

We made our way among the souls oppressed
And bent beneath the rain, and trod upon
Their emptiness which seems like living flesh.
Around and under they lay on the ground   35
Save only one, who, as we passed along
Caught sight of us and stirred to sit upright.
"You there, conducted through this world of Hell,"
He called out, "recognize me if you can,
For you were made before I was undone."   40
I answered him: "The anguish of your pain,
It may be, drives remembrance from my mind,
So to my thinking we have never met.
But tell me who you are that find yourself
In such a sorry spot and so distressed?   45
Worse punishments there may be; none more foul."

He answered: "Your own city, with the gall
Of envy overflowing, counted me
Among its dwellers in the life serene.
Your townsmen called me Ciacco. Here I pay   50
The fee of gluttony, injurious fault;
Sodden and helpless, as you see, I lie.
Nor does my misery lack for company;
A like reward falls on all hereabout
For like transgression." And he said no more.   55
Whereat I further: "Ciacco, your sad state
Affects me so that I am moved to tears.
But tell me, if you can, what lies in store
For those who dwell in our divided city,
Why is it plagued by discord, and with truth   60
Can any of its townsmen be called just?"

And he made answer: "After long dispute
They'll come to bloodshed and the rural party

44

Your townsmen called me Ciacco.   *Inferno* VI, 50

Will drive the other out with great offense.
Later 't will be the former's turn to fall   65
Within three suns, and the other's to arise
Armed with the strength of him who straddles now.
These then for long shall bear their foreheads high,
Crushing the other side beneath great weights
Whoever may feel grief or shame thereby.   70
Two just men are there – neither of them heeded.
Pride, envy, avarice; it's these that are
The three brands that have fired every heart."
He ended here his melancholy sound.

Then I to him, "I'd have you teach me more   75
And grant me guerdon of yet further speech.
Farinata and Tegghiaio, worthy men,
Jacopo Rusticucci, Arrigo and Mosca,
And others who employed their gifts for good,
Tell me, where are they now? How shall I know them?   80
For great desire presses me to learn
If they share sweet of Heaven or gall of Hell."
And he: "They lie among the blacker souls
And divers guilts press them yet deeper down;
If you descend so far you may behold them.   85
But when you are once more in the sweet world,
Recall me, pray, to others' memory.
I'll say no more. I'll answer you no more."

His glance he turned and, eyeing me askance
But briefly, he then downward bent his head   90
And like the others sagged beneath the hail.
Then said my chief: "No more will he arise
Until the blast of the angelic horn
Announce the coming of the adverse host.

Then will each one revisit his sad tomb   95
And take again his figure and his flesh
And learn his sentence through eternity."

So we passed on with heavy steps amidst
The vague and shadowy shapes and the dull rain,
Touching somewhat upon the life to come.   100
"These torments, master," thus I questioned him,
"When judgment day is past, will they increase
Or grow less painful or remain the same?"
He answered me: "Your *Science* read once more,
And therein learn how, as perfection grows,   105
So is the substance better shaped to sense
Its good or evil. And although the damned
To true perfection never come, yet after
They will be nearer to it than before."

We edged the marge of that dark circle's rim,   110
With further comment that I here omit,
And reached at length the path that, leading down,
With hostile Plutus brought us face to face.

CANTO VII

Plutus.   *Inferno* VII, 2

"Papè Satan, Papè Satan, Aleppe,"
So Plutus stuttered, clucking in our path,
And my all-knowing sage to soothe me said:
"Be not distressed by fear, no strength of his
Suffices to forbid us the descent."   5
Addressing then those peevish swollen lips
He cried: "No more from you, accursed wolf;
Digest within yourself your bitter bile.
Not without cause we visit the abyss;
Our warrant's from above where Michael wrought   10
A sharp revenge on rebel insolence."
As sails the breath of wind has bellied out
Fall in a tangled mass when the mast cracks,
So down in swift collapse the monster dropped.

Thus deeper did we pierce the rugged gulch   15
Enfolding all the evil of the world,
And in the fourth entrenchment stayed our steps.
Justice Divine, who could enumerate
The new travails and pains I witnessed here?
And why must our own sinning waste us so?   20
Even as the wave that by Charybdis roaring
Rolls on to break against opposing surge,
Such was the style of contradancing here.
On either hand my eyes beheld a horde
More numerous than elsewhere, each side bent   25
To roll with straining muscles massive weights
Against the other, shouting as they toiled.
Crashing together the opposing bands
Would turn about and roll their burdens back,
Crying, "What profits spending?" "What price thrift?"   30
And so they plodded round the dreary ring,
Each crew on its own cycle, each to each

49

Forever calling out the shameful taunt
Until, the semicircular tour complete,
Again they clashed and cried and turned again.   35

And I, with heart near moved to sympathy,
"Tell me, O master, who are these?" I asked.
"Are these all clerics, tonsured, on our left?"
He made reply: "In former life they all
So squint-eyed looked on reason that their goods   40
With no right measure were expended. So
Their mutual reproach barks out their shame
As they confront each other on their rounds,
Which they must tread for opposite excess.
Clerics were these who wear no hairy thatch   45
Upon their head – aye, Popes and Cardinals,
Among whom greed attains its grade supreme."
"Among them, master, I should recognize
Some who were marred by this defect," I said.
"In vain you cherish hope," the answer came,   50
"The unperceptive life that stained their souls
Here makes them dark to all identity.
Eternally this butting will go on;
One company will rise on judgment day
With folded fist, the other with shorn locks.   55
Ill hoarding and ill spending has deprived
These sinners of the light and placed them here
Thus stupidly to brawl, as you perceive:
Their plight needs no adornment of my words.
Now you may see, my son, how short-lived are   60
The empty winnings of the game men play
With goods of Fortune for which they contend,
For all the gold there is or ever was
Beneath the moon could buy no mite of rest
For any one of these exhausted souls."   65

And, happy as all Primal Creatures are,
She rolls her sphere, contented in her bliss.

Inferno VII, 95–96

"This Fortune, master mine, whereof you speak,"
I then inquired, "who is she, that she holds
All worldly goods so firmly in her grasp?"
He then to me: "O silly race of men,
What monstrous ignorance wreaks you such ill!   70
Now listen and digest my lesson well.
He whose transcendent mind embraces all
Made the wide wheeling spheres and to each one
Assigned its guardian, that with radiance
Reciprocal each ring might shine, its light   75
Reflecting equally on sister spheres.
And likewise, for the splendors of your world,
A minister and viceroy he ordained
Whose charge is timely changing of vain wealth
Ever from folk to folk, from clan to clan,   80
Beyond prevision of all human schemes.
Wherefore one people rules, another serves,
In harmony with her divine decree
Which, like a snake in the grass, moves unperceived.
Your human wit may not withstand her will;   85
Hers to provide and hers to make awards,
In her sphere sovereign like the other gods.
Her permutations know no pause, for those
Whose turn is come so thickly press on her
That of necessity she deals with speed.   90
This then is she who is so pilloried
And falsely blamed and spitefully accursed
By those same folk that should her praises sing.
But in her blessedness she hears them not,
And, happy as all Primal Creatures are,   95
She rolls her sphere, contented in her bliss.
Now let us downward toward a greater grief;
The stars now turn to setting that arose
When I came forth and we must not delay."

Cutting the circle to its inner edge   100
We came upon a spring that, boiling forth,
Flows downward through a channel it has carved.
Darker than perse the waters of that stream,
And we, in company with its blackish flow,
Moved downward by a strange and tortuous trail.   105

The gloomy streamlet when it comes to rest
Below the grey and sinister ravine
Expands into a marsh that is called Styx.
There, casting forth a scrutinizing glance,
I saw a muddy tribe in that morass,   110
All naked and resentful in their scowls.
There were they brawling, not with hands alone
Striking each other, but with head and chest
And kicking feet, and rending with their teeth.
Here spoke my kindly master: "Now, my son,   115
Behold the souls whom anger overcame.
Under the water too, I'd have you know,
Others are deep submerged and with their gasps
Send bubbles to the surface of this ooze,
As glancing roundabout you may observe.   120
Fixed in the slime they say: 'Sullen we were
In the sweet air cheered by the brightening sun
Because of sulky vapors in our hearts;
Now here in this black mulch we curse our luck.'
This burden, though they cannot form in words,   125
They gargle in their gullets."
                              Then between
The marsh and the dry bank we made an arc
About the filthy pond, with eyes intent
On the mud-swallowers therein submerged,
Coming at last to rest beneath a tower.   130

52

CANTO VIII

As one who, learning of some monstrous trick
Played on him, shows resentment, even so
Phlegyas became in his swift mounting rage.

Inferno VIII, 21–23

Now to resume: before we stood beneath
The lofty tower our glance had climbed its height,
Following two torches that we saw placed there.
Another distant gleamed as in response
So brightly as to fix my eye on it.   5
To my lord, sea of wisdom, turning then
I asked: "What are those beacons? Why replies
The other torch and who directs their beams?"
He answered me: "Across the sordid creek,
If mist of this morass conceal him not,   10
You may espy the envoy summoned hither."
Never did arrow leave the bended bow
So speedily to whistle through the air
As at that moment I beheld a skiff
Skim o'er the water toward us, swift propelled   15
By one sole oarsman, crying as he rowed,
"O vicious soul, now are you come indeed!"
"O Phlegyas, Phlegyas, empty is your threat,"
My master answered, "this time we are yours
No longer than the crossing may require."   20
As one who, learning of some monstrous trick
Played on him, shows resentment, even so
Phlegyas became in his swift mounting rage.
My captain then stepped down into the skiff,
Bidding me sit beside him. Only then   25
Did the small craft seem laden, and as soon
As we had come aboard, my chief and I,
The ancient prow took off, cutting the waves
More deeply than its wont with other freight.

As we were ferried o'er the stagnant pool   30
A head was thrust up, all befouled with mud,
And questioned: "Who are you that come before

Your time?" "I come but do not stay," I said;
"Say, rather, who are you, so much befouled?"
He answered: "One in tears, as you may see."   35
And I to him: "Let weeping and remorse
Be still your lot, O soul accurst, for well
I recognize you, filthy as you are."
Whereat he stretched out both his arms toward us
And my perceptive master pushed him back,   40
Crying, "Be off now, with the other curs."
And then he threw his arms around my neck
And kissed my face and said: "O haughty soul,
Blessed be she in whom you were conceived.
This wretch was proud and insolent in life;   45
No kindly act redeems his memory,
And hence in anger here his shadow lies.
How many in the light of day comport
Themselves like kings who here below like pigs
Will wallow in the muck, and leave behind   50
Contempt abysmal in the minds of men."
"Master," I said, "I would be pleased to see
Him deeply sunken in this scummy broth
Before we leave the lake." And he replied,
"It shall be done before we see the shore,   55
For right it is that you be satisfied."
And thereupon my eager eyes beheld
Such treatment dealt him by his muddy mates
For which I still thank God and praise His name.
"After Filippo Argenti!" was the cry;   60
The waspish spirit of the Florentine
For very rage did turn and bite himself.
We left him thus; I tell no more of him.

A sound of moaning from across the gulf
Struck on my ear, so that with gaze intent   65

I peered ahead. "My son," the master said,
"Now we approach the dreadful town of Dis,
With its sad citizens and direful host."
I answered: "In the valley I discern
Its mosques vermilion as though bathed in fire."   70
And he rejoined: "The everlasting heat
Burning within this lower reach of Hell
Gives them the ruddy hue that you remark."
Meanwhile into the deeper moat we came
Which girds that desolate city round about;   75
Above us loomed its iron-colored walls.
Some time we skirted its forbidding side
Until our boatman called in accents loud:
"Here stands the entrance. Go ashore."
                                    Atop
The gates score upon score I saw of those   80
By Heaven rejected. Fiercely they began:
"Who is this rash one, paying not death's fee,
That dares to penetrate into his realm?"
At this my master wise made sign to show
He would have secret parley with them. Then,   85
Their wrath somewhat abating, they called out:
"Come you alone to speak with us, but he
Who has so rashly trespassed in this land,
Let his steps now retrace their foolish path –
If he can find the way – while you, his guide   90
Through this dark country, may remain with us."

Think for yourself, O reader, what dismay
Lay hold on me when these grim words I heard,
Fearing forever hopeless my return.
"Dearest my lord, who seven times and more   95
Have been my shield 'gainst every peril faced,

57

Leave me not now all helpless in this strait.
If further progress be denied to us,
Together let us backward turn at once."
He then who thus far had escorted me   100
Made answer: "Do not be afraid; no-one
May bar our way, such warrant is given us.
Await me here and your dejected heart
Comfort and nourish with the food of hope.
I'll not desert you in this nether world."   105
Then he who was as father dear to me
Went off and left me in my soul perplexed
As hope and fear debated in my mind.
I could not hear what he proposed to them,
But brief and futile was their colloquy.   110
Our adversaries broke and ran pell mell
Behind the gates and shut them in the face
Of my good lord who, left outside alone,
Turned back to me with slow and heavy stride.
His gaze was downcast and his brow was razed   115
Of confidence, and, sighing, he complained:
"Who has the dolorous city barred from us?"
And turning then to me, "Be not dismayed
By my concern for I shall win the test,
Whatever the defenders plot within.   120
This is no recent arrogance of theirs;
At a less secret gate it once was shown
Which ever since has hung on shattered hinge;
I mean that gate whereon you read the scroll
Portentous. And from there even now one comes   125
Alone down the decline through all the rings,
Of such a nature that upon his touch
Our entrance will be granted unopposed."

CANTO IX

The pallor fright depicted on my face
When I beheld my master turn, rebuffed,
Caused him his own new color to repress.
As one with ear alert he stood intent,
For sight had little power to penetrate   5
The heavy air by marsh-mist overlaid.
"And yet," he thus began, "the victory
Must fall to us, unless – such aid was pledged . . .
Ah, how this waiting irks me till he come."
I well observed how his speech covered up   10
Its first beginnings with an after phrase
Of different sense from what had gone before,
Yet none the less I felt the grasp of fear,
Drawing, it may be, from his hesitance
A worse conclusion than he had conceived.   15
"Down to this dismal depth of Hell's abyss
Comes ever any soul of the first ring
Whose only penalty is hope denied?"
This question I put forth and he replied:
"Seldom it is that any one of us   20
Takes up the trail on which I lead you now;
However, I myself came once before.
Erichtho cruel, whose black arts could recall
The parted soul to its forsaken bones
Conjured me forth. The mantle of the flesh   25
I had but freshly laid aside when she
Sent me to seek a shade from Judas' seat.
That is the lowest and the darkest spot
Of Hell's whole chasm and the most remote
From highest wheeling heaven. Hence the road   30
Is not unknown to me; be comforted.
This swamp exhaling overwhelming stench
Girds all about the inner town of woe,

61

Where now we may not enter save by force."
And more he said that I did not retain,   35
For my attention, following my gaze,
Was turned to the high towers' crimson crest
Where suddenly three Furies stood in sight,
Hell-nurtured creatures, stained with blood. In shape
And gesture women they appeared, begirt   40
With hissing snakes of brightly gleaming green;
In place of tresses round their temples writhed
Cerastes and small serpents set to strike.
Then he who recognized the attendant maids
Of deathless sorrow's Empress, said to me: 45
"Mark there the vengeful Furies: on the left
Megaera, wailing on her right behold
Alecto, dread Tisiphone between
Her fearful sisters stands." Each ghoulish witch
Was rending with sharp talons her own breast.   50
Their clawlike hands they clapped with such shrill screams
That numb with fear I held close to the bard.
"Now let Medusa come and make him stone,"
They cried out, bending down their evil glance,
"For ill we did to suffer unavenged   55
The assault of Theseus." "Quick," my master said,
"Cover your face and turn your back on them,
For should the Gorgon come and meet your eye
Vain would be any hope of your return."
And as he spoke he turned me round about   60
And placed his own hands firmly over mine
For safer hiding of my frightened eyes.

O you who healthy intellect possess,
Consider well the doctrine here concealed
Under the pregnant veiling of my verse.   65

Where suddenly three Furies stood in sight,
Hell-nurtured creatures, stained with blood.

Inferno ix, 38–39

While yet he spoke, across the turbid stream
A crashing sound was heard so ominous
That shudders shook the shadowed riverbanks,
Alike to when a wind impetuous,
Whipped to a fury by conflicting heats,   70
Falls on the forest and without restraint
Uproots great trunks and bears the branches off,
And, dust encircled, sweeps on in its pride,
Driving before it shepherds and their flocks.
"Look yonder," Virgil cried, and freed my eyes,   75
"Across the ancient flood where vapors rise
Most thickly." And, as in a pond the frogs
Leap wide and plunge aside in frightened flight
Before the questing snake until at last
They squat together on the riverbed,   80
So here more than a thousand I beheld
Of souls forsaken flee the fleet approach
Of one who fared, dry-footed, 'cross the Styx.
Moving his left hand free before his face
He brushed aside the fetid atmosphere;   85
Untroubled, save for that, he trod serene.
I knew him for a heavenly messenger
And to my master turned; he made a sign
That I should speak no word but only kneel.

Wearing an aspect of supreme disdain   90
He reached the gate and with his little wand
But touched it, and forthwith it opened wide.
"O wretched company, outcasts of Heaven,"
So on that dreadful threshold he began,
"Whence springs this futile arrogance of yours?   95
Whence this recalcitrance against that will
Whose purpose may brook no impediment?"

Have you not learned that superadded woe
Is certain payment for your insolence?
What boots it to butt goatlike against fate?   100
Bethink you how your warden Cerberus
Still bears a lacerated throat and jaw."
Over the Stygian path he turned back then,
Sparing no word for us, but with the mien
Of one whose mind is fixed on other things   105
Than those before him.
                                            Toward the city gate
After his holy words we went secure.
We entered and no further hindrance found;
And I, once in, looked closely all about,
Eager to learn the lot of those immured   110
Within the fortress. I beheld a plain
Bestrewn with tokens of deep suffering
And bitter torments. As beside the walls
Of Arles where mighty Rhône the marshland floods,
Or hard by Pola, where Quarnero flows   115
To seal the limits of our Italy,
The plains are checkered here and there with tombs
So was it here, save that the manner was
More sinister, for 'midst the sepulchres
Fires burned incessant and the caskets glowed   120
Like iron ready for the blacksmith's stroke.

The coffins stood uncovered; from them poured
Such anguished groans as terribly revealed
The sufferings of the tortured souls within.
I asked: "What sinners buried in yon chests   125
Put forth such lamentations, though unseen?"
"The chieftains of the sects heretical
With all their schools," my master answered me.

64

"Now let Medusa come and make him stone."

Inferno IX, 53

"These tombs are richer in their wicked spoil
Than you may credit. Like entombed with like   130
Here lie, with variation in the heat
To suit the sin." Then, bearing to the right,
We strode between the torments and the wall.

I knew him for a heavenly messenger.

Inferno IX, 87

CANTO X

Now by a hidden path that ran between
The city walls and torture tombs my guide
Betook himself, and I upon his heels.
I spoke: "Virtue supreme, that at your will
Conduct me through this evil labyrinth,   5
I pray you, satisfy my sharp desire;
May we not see who lie within the tombs?
No guard stands by and every lid is raised."
He answered: "When these heretics retrieve
Their mortal spoils abandoned up above   10
And hear the judgment of Jehoshaphat
Then will each tomb be sealed for evermore.
On this side Epicurus and his train
Have sepulchre, they who affirmed the soul
Dies with the flesh. But touching your request   15
Herein shall you be shortly satisfied,
And your unspoken wish shall be fulfilled."
"My lord," I said, "My heart hides naught from you;
I sought not subterfuge but brevity.
Ere now commended by your sage advice."   20

"O Tuscan who walk living through the fire
Of our grim city, uttering honest speech,
Pause, if it please you, briefly where you stand.
Your language to my ear proclaims you one
Born in that noble fatherland which I   25
Perhaps too harshly dealt with." On my ear
All unexpecting came this sally forth
From the hot tombs, whereat I drew myself,
Affrighted, closer to my leader's side.
"What means this? Turn about!" he chided me.   30
"Behold how Farinata all upright
From breast to head emerges from his fire."

69

Already were my eyes drawn to his mien
While he stood, chest outthrust and haughty-browed
As if all Hell he held in vast contempt.   35
Meanwhile my captain's eager hands thrust me
Between the sepulchres before his presence
With cautioning counsel: "Count your words with care."

Before the tomb I stood; sharply he glanced
And queried almost angrily of me: 40
"Who were your elders?" Eager to obey
I freely spoke and nothing did conceal.
Whereat he, lifting higher still his brow:
"Sworn enemies they were to me and mine
And to my party; twice I drove them forth."   45
"If they were thrust out they came back again,"
I answered, "from all quarters, aye, both times;
An art your partisans have never learned."
Hereat another shade beside him rose,
Only the head revealed above the tomb;   50
(He'd raised himself upon his knees, I think.)
He looked around me, trying, as it seemed
To see if there were not another with me,
But when his circumspection was complete
In tears he spoke: "If lofty genius grants   55
You passage through this blinded prison, why
Stands not my son beside you? Where is he?"
I made reply: "Through merit of my own
I came not hither; he who yonder waits
Is sponsor for me. Guido, it may be,   60
Held him not in the proper reverence."
(His plaint and fashion of his penalty
Identified him; hence was my reply
So full and clear.) Incontinent he rose

70

Ritratto degli Uomini X

BASKIN
1960

While he stood, chest outthrust and haughty-browed
As if all Hell he held in vast contempt.

Inferno x, 34-35

And cried out: "You say 'held'? What then, he lives   65
No more? No longer his dear eyes drink in
The sweet light of the warm life-giving sun?"
Then, marking how I halted in reply,
He fell supine nor reappeared again.

But that great-hearted one at whose behest   70
I had first stopped had altered not his mien,
Nor even so much as turned his neck or side,
But spoke in sharp rebuttal to my thrust:
"If my folk leave that lesson still unlearned
It more torments me than this bed of mine.   75
How bitter is the schooling in that skill
You too will know, yea, even before the queen
Here regnant fifty times renew her glow.
But as you cherish hope to see again
The fair earth overhead, disclose to me   80
Why such remorseless foes to all my kin
Your people show themselves in every law."
"The slaughter and the carnage," I replied,
"That colored Arbia's waters with our blood
Calls forth such vengeful prayers at our shrines."   85
Sighing he shook his head and made reply:
"There I was not alone, nor certainly
Would I have joined the others without cause.
But all alone I stood when every one
Was ready to raze Florence to the ground,   90
There did I only openly defend her."
"So may your seed find rest at last from strife,"
I asked him, "solve this knot for me, I pray,
Which holds my concept tangled in its web:
If I hear rightly, you who dwell below   95
Have sense of things not yet matured by time,

While of the present you are unaware."
"As in a faltering light we may discern,"
He answered, "the crude shape of things to come;
So much is granted us by Power supreme.   100
But matters near at hand or in their course
Are out of our perception. If none come
To bear us tidings nothing do we know
Of mortal things. Thus you may understand
All knowledge will be closed to us when once   105
The gate of mankind's future is sealed up."

At this, now conscious of my fault, I said:
"Inform your comrade, stricken low by grief,
That his son still is counted 'mongst the quick,
And that my answer came not readily   110
Because of false opinion of your sight,
Which now your explanation has corrected."

My master had already urged me on,
So hastily I asked of that great shade
What sinners dwelt with him. He briefly said: 115
"More than a thousand souls lie here with me:
The Second Frederick and the Cardinal,
With more who shall be nameless." He withdrew,
And I, made pensive by his prophecy
Boding me ill, rejoined the ancient bard.   120
He started off and as he strode along
He queried: "Why so downcast?" I at once
Set forth in full the cause of my concern.
"Bear well within your mind what you have learned
Of cares to come," the sage admonished me,   125
"And heed me here." Then, with his finger raised:
"When you shall stand before the loving glance

Of one whose eyes see all, from her you'll learn
The pattern of the journey of your life."
Then, veering from the wall and to the left, 130
We followed, towards the center of the town,
A pathway winding downward to a vale
Which high above sent forth its filthy stench.

CANTO XI

Upon the very brink of a high bank
Made by a circle of huge broken rocks
We came upon a yet more fearful pack,
And here, because of the intolerable stench
Thrown upward from the yawning pit below,   5
We drew back, taking refuge against the lid
Of a great tomb whereon I saw inscribed:
"I hold the soul of Anastasius, Pope,
Led by Photinus from the rightful path."

"Here we must slow the pace of our descent   10
And first allow our sense to grow accustomed
To the foul air, then we shall scarcely heed it."
So spoke the master. I replied, "Pray find
Some recompense, so our time may not pass
Wasted." And he: "Mark you, such is my thought."   15

"My son, within the compass of these rocks,"
Thus he began his discourse, "are three rings,
From rank to lower rank, like those you are leaving.
And all of them are full of cursed spirits,
But, so that henceforth mere sight may suffice,   20
Learn how and why they are in such constraint.
Of every malice earning Heaven's hate
The end is injury, and every such intent
Through either force or fraud brings hurt to others.
Since fraud however is man's special vice   25
It most displeases God, wherefore the guileful
Are lowest down and greater woe assails them.
The violent possess the whole first ring
But since force may be used against three persons
It is constructed of three separate zones.   30
Force may be used 'gainst God, oneself, one's neighbor,

77

Either toward them or things pertaining to them,
As you will hear in open exposition.
Upon one's neighbor murder may be wrought
And grievous wounds, and against what is his   35
Spoilage and arson and unrighteous tolls.
So murderers, those guilty of assault,
Spoilers and robbers, each in his own group,
Are all tormented in the upper ring.
One may turn violent hand against oneself   40
Or one's estate, so in the second round
Whoever of your world himself deprives
Or dissipates and wastes his goods must grieve
Repentant now to no avail, and weeps
Instead of being joyful as he should.   45
One may use force against the deity,
Denying in one's heart or cursing Him,
Or scorning Nature and her bounteous works
Wherefore the smallest ring seals with its stamp
Both Sodom and Cahors and those as well   50
Who speak forth, scorning God within their hearts.
Now fraud, whereof each conscience feels the bite,
May be employed against those who trust the cheater
Or such as have no special cause for faith.
This second fashion, it is clear, destroys   55
Only the bond of love that nature makes;
So in the second circle find their nests
Hypocrisy, flattery, and sorcerers,
And falsehood, thievery and simony,
And go-betweens and grafters and like filth.   60
In the first manner, that love is forgotten
Which nature makes and the additional bond
That is the source of special confidence.
So in the lowest ring where lies the point

Simony.   *Inferno* XI, 59

Of the universe whereover Dis is built   65
All traitors are eternally consumed."
I answered, "Master, your discourse proceeds
Most clearly and most excellently defines
This cavern and the people it contains.
But tell me now – those of the sodden swamp,   70
Or those wind-driven, or beaten by the rain,
And those who meet exchanging bitter words –
Why are not they within the fiery city
Punished likewise if God holds them in wrath?
And if He does not – how explain their plight?"   75
He answered, "Why goes wandering your wit
So widely from its wont? Or whereon, say
Does your mind fix its glance? Nay, do you not
Recall those words in which your *Ethics* treats
Of the three dispositions Heaven holds   80
All unacceptable: incontinence
And malice and insensate beastliness?
And how incontinence of all the three
Offends God least and incurs least of blame?
If you examine well this statement, and   85
Call to your memory who such sinners are
Suffering their penance here outside the walls
You'll soon see clearly why they stand apart
From the rogues I've cited and why with lesser ire
The hammer of God's vengeance bludgeons them."   90
"O sun that heals all clouded sight, so much
Content you bring me when you solve my problems
That doubting pleases me no less than knowing.
But now, pray turn you back somewhat to where
You were remarking how usury offends   95
Goodness divine; untie that knot for me."
"Philosophy, for those who read aright,

Takes note," he said, "and not in one part only,
How nature charts her course from the divine
Intelligence and from its operation,   100
And if you will peruse your *Physics* well
You will observe, after not many pages,
That human art, so far as it is able,
Like pupil after master, follows nature
So that your art is, as it were, God's grandchild.   105
And from these twain, if you but call to mind
Genesis and its first chapters, mankind must
Draw forth its living and prosperity.
The usurer, choosing another way
Doubly despises nature in itself   110
And in its follower, placing hope elsewhere.
But come now, follow, for I would go on;
The Fish are flickering over the horizon
And above Caurus hovers high the wain.
And farther onward lies the cliff's descent."   115

CANTO XII

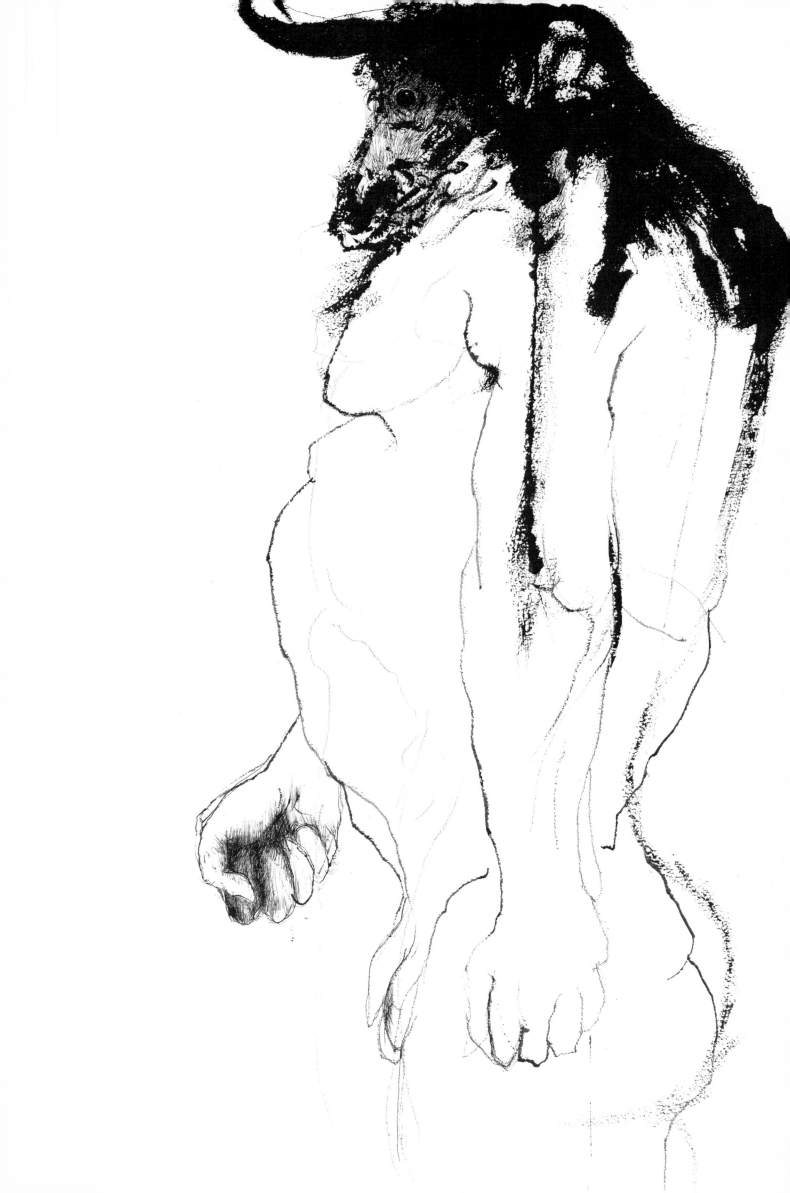

Barred by such a monstrous sight
As travelers would tremble to confront.

Inferno XII, 2–3

Where our descent began the craggy path
Was steep and barred by such a monstrous sight
As travelers would tremble to confront.
As is the land-slip somewhat south of Trent
Carved out by Adige, either through fault   5
Of fissured earth or by a tremor racked,
Where some rough footing might the rock afford
To one who sought a pathway from the crest,
Of like construction was our passage here;
And, on the summit of the jagged stair,   10
The bestial shame of Crete, conceived within
The wooden cow, lay waiting. When he marked
Our near approach he bit himself for rage,
As one nigh maddened by an inner ire.
"Perhaps you think the Duke of Athens come,"   15
My sage called to him, "he who was your death.
Aside, dumb beast, this wayfarer comes not
Instructed by your sister to your ill,
But rather seeking knowledge of your woes."
Even as the steer who shakes his rope aside   20
As the axe falls and, dying on his feet,
No longer walks but random leaps and bounds,
So did the Minotaur while Virgil cried,
"Run to the pass; go down while yet he raves."
In this wise did we downward make our way   25
Over the rough shale, which beneath the weight
Of living tread gave passage insecure.

I walked on bowed in thought. The poet spoke:
"You meditate, it may be, on the cleft
Whereon the wrathful beast stands sentinel   30
Whom I frustrated. On my last descent
To plumb the nether depths of Hell this rock

83

Was not yet split. But some time, I recall,
Before His coming who the lofty train
Released from Limbo, this whole fetid vale   35
Gave forth a shudder and the universe,
I thought, felt love – for there are those who hold
The force of love makes chaos of the world.
Then was it that this old primaeval rock
Both here and elsewhere fissured and collapsed.   40
But downward bend your gaze for we approach
The steaming crimson flood wherein immersed
Are they whose blood-lust has oppressed mankind."

O greed unseeing, violence insane,
So spurring us to ill in this short life,   45
So drowning us for all eternity!

I saw a river wide, with its full arch
Encircling the plain beneath the rock,
As my escort had told me, and in file
Between the hillside and the rocky banks   50
Swift centaurs galloped, armed with ready bows,
As on the earth of old they used to hunt.

They halted one and all as we came on,
Then three detached themselves from the patrol
With bow in hand and arrows to the strings.   55
While yet afar one challenged: "You two, there;
What is your pain assigned? Stand where you are
And speak. Come nearer and this arrow flies."
"Chiron will hear our answer," said my lord,
"As always, too hot hasty is your mood."   60
Then, nudging me, he whispered: "Nessus, he,
Whom love of Dejanira led to death

84

And who prepared his own vendetta. Next
To him stands Chiron, with his head bowed low,
And close beside stands Pholus, once so wrathful.   65
Around the riverbank they swarm in hordes,
Transfixing with their shafts whoever dares
Emerge from out the stream more than his due."

As we came nearer to those creatures fleet
Chiron took up a bolt and with the notch   70
Parted his beard and smoothed it on his cheek.
Uncovering thus his ample mouth for speech,
He uttered to his mates: "Mark you, how he,
The second one, moves pebbles with his feet?
The disembodied shades have no such strength."   75
My master, nearing him, stood at his chest
Where human breast and equine frame conjoined
And answered; "Aye, a lonely mortal he
In this dark vale wherein it is my charge
To shepherd him. Necessity compels   80
His journey here, not idle whim, for she
Who set me on my task did interrupt
Her happy sharing in the heavenly choir
To seek me out in Limbo for his guide.
Here have you none apt for the boiling stream;   85
No bandit he, nor lying soul am I.
Nay rather, by the virtue which empowers
My steps to move across this wilderness,
Lend us an escort to reveal the ford
And one to bear this man upon his back,   90
Since man he is and has not wings to fly."

Addressing Nessus, who stood on his right,
Chiron commanded: "Back with them and lead

85

These twain as they request. Should any squad
Obstruct your passage, bid them turn aside." 95
So with our faithful convoy we set off
Along the shore that flanked the scarlet stream,
The boiling wretches crying in our ears.
Some saw I all blood-covered to the brow,
Of whom the Centaur said: "All tyrants, these, 100
Whose cruel and predatory hands were laid
On subjects and their chattels. Here they mourn
Their bloody booty. Alexander groans,
And Dionysius answers for the years
Of cruel despotism in Sicily. 105
You see that sullen visage, darkly browed?
'Tis Azzolino, and close by him stands
The blond Opizzo, who, to tell the tale
Aright, was strangled by his bastard son."
I eyed my master who made answer: "Here 110
I am your second mentor, he the first."

We moved on further till the Centaur stopped
Above a folk that from the seething pool
A full head could project. He showed us one
Who stood apart, and said: "In God's own sight 115
This killer stabbed the kingly heart that still
Is held in reverence beside the Thames."
Onward we went, and some I saw who stood
With head and chest above the steaming blood,
And many of those souls I recognized. 120
With each successive step the blood-red stream
Subsided, till the sinners last in line
Stood from the ankle free. Here was our ford.
The man-horse spoke again: "As here you see
The boiling bath grow shallow, so it slopes 125

From here on ever deeper till it reaches
Where tyranny in anguish is submerged.
God's justice here forever scourges him
Who was the scourge of nations, Attila,
With Pyrrhus, Sextus Pompey and their like.   130
The two Rinieris, bandits both, with tears
Milked by God's wrath, pay fee for fearful crimes
Upon the highways." Here his lesson ceased
And leaving us he sped across the ford.

CANTO XIII

Scarcely had Nessus reached the other shore
When we moved onward through a wilderness
Whose tangled brush no trail or pathway cut;
Its somber shade no verdant leaf relieved,
Nor shapely branches, and the knotted trunks,   5
Contorted, bore no fruit but poisoned stalks.
The savage beasts that by Corneto dwell,
Contemptuous of cultivated fields,
Have no more dense nor thornier abode.
Here the foul Harpies build their noisome nests,   10
Who with bleak portents of dire ills to come
Drove out the Trojans from the Strophades.
Man-like in neck and face, they have wide wings,
Clawed feet and swollen bellies plumed. They perch
Upon the tortured boughs and mouth laments.   15
"Before proceeding," my good master said,
"Know that you now are in the second round,
And will remain in it until you come
Into the region of the dreadful sand.
Look closely here and you will witness things   20
That you would hardly credit from my lips."
On every side outcries of woe I heard
Without perceiving whence could be their source,
Wherefore, confused, I faltered in my stride.
I think that he was thinking that I thought   25
Such voices issued from among the trunks,
The utterance of folk concealed from us,
On which account he said: "If you break off
Some twig of those projecting from these plants
Conclusion of your fancy will be lopped."   30
Then I stretched out my hand and plucked a shoot,
And from the trunk came forth: "Why mangle me?"
(Dark blood discolored it as the words came.)

"Have you no pity that you rend me so?
Men were we once who here are but bare boughs;   35
Yet had we serpents been even so your hand
Might well have been more gentle in its touch."

As a green log that burning on the hearth
At one end smokes and from the other drips
And hisses as the air escapes in sighs,   40
So from this broken wood alike came forth
Blood drops and words. I let the splinter fall
And stood as one in fright. My sage replied:
"If earlier he could but have believed,
O wounded soul, what only in my verse   45
He had encountered, then he had not raised
His hand to hurt you. But so past belief
Is your state here that I was led to urge
On him the act that I myself regret.
Tell him now who you were so that in place   50
Of compensation here he may refresh
Your fame on earth where he will soon return."

The trunk replied: "Your blandishments so tempt me
I can't keep mute; may it not weary you
If my words for a while hold me ensnared.   55
I am the one who held both of the keys
To Frederick's heart and, locking or unlocking,
I could so smoothly turn them that I kept
Almost all others from his confidence.
Such loyalty I practiced in my task   60
That sleep and health I sacrificed to it.
That courtesan who never yet has turned
Her meretricious eyes from Caesar's court –
That common death, that curse of courtiers –

92

Inflamed against me each and every mind   65
And they, inflamed, inflamed Augustus too,
So my bright honors turned to sad regrets.
My soul then, by disdainful passion moved,
Thinking through death I might escape disdain
Made me unrighteous toward my righteous self.   70
But by the new roots of this tree I swear
That never in my life did I break faith
With my lord who so well deserved high honor.
Should one of you twain go back to the world
Let him restore the memory of me,   75
Still lying prostrate under Envy's blow."

After a little pause the poet spoke:
"Now that his tale is told, ask what you will;
Speak now, nor let the right occasion pass."
I answered: "Such compassion clogs my tongue   80
Words will not come; since you know my desire
I pray you query him on my behalf."
The courteous bard then of the shade enquired,
"So freely may be granted your request,
Instruct us, if it please you, how the soul   85
Is fused within the boughs, and if it be
That ever any spirit finds release."
Then from the branch a murmurous rustling came
From which emerged these words in human speech:
"You shall have answer given in few words: 90
When the ferocious spirit leaves behind
The body from which it has torn itself,
Minos directs it to the seventh gulf;
It falls into the wood, no place is fixed
But there wherever chance may fling it down   95
It germinates even as a grain of spelt,

And grows into a seedling, a wild plant.
The Harpies come and, feeding on its leaves,
Give at once pain and portal for the pain.
We'll seek, as will the rest, our spoils – but not   100
To clothe ourselves again for it's not right
That one reclaim what he has cast away.
Hither we'll drag them; thenceforth through the bleak
Wasteland will hang our bodies, each attached
To the thorn tree of its obnoxious shade."   105

While yet we waited on his further words
A crashing in the woods came to our ears,
As to one posted for the hunted boar
There comes the thrashing of the quarry mixed
With hunters' shouts and crackling underbrush.   110
And lo! in panic flight from off the left
Two naked lacerated fugitives
Rushed by and trampled the impeding bush.
He in the lead cried out: "O come, Death, come!"
His fellow, as though grieved to be outstripped,   115
Panted behind him: "Lano, not so fast
Were your untutored strides at Toppo's joust."
Whereat with breath all spent he stumbled down
And huddled close behind a bushy clump.
Hard on their heels the dark wood seemed to swarm   120
With fleet hound-bitches, black and fast and keen
As harriers fresh unleased upon their prey.
On him who squatted low they turned their fangs
And rending him apart they carried off
The bleeding limbs still living in their pain.   125

As they withdrew my escort took my hand
And led me to the bush which dripped hot tears

94

And led me to the bush which dripped hot tears
Through every mangled shoot.

Inferno XIII, 127–128

Through every mangled shoot and cried aloud:
"O Giácomo, what did it profit you,
Seeking to use my branches as a shield?   130
Why must I share in payment of your guilt?"
Standing above, my master questioned him:
"Who once were you whose protest is breathed forth
Mingled with blood?" He answered us: "O souls
Who have beheld the cruelty undeserved   135
That reft my leafage from me, I implore
Your charity; pray gather up the shoots
And lay them 'neath my mutilated trunk.
My birth was in that town that chose to take
The Baptist for her second patron, whence   140
The first, resentful, with his martial arts
Forever brings her misery. If some trace
Of ancient cult of him did not still stand
Where Arno's shores are spanned, those citizens
Who built anew what Attila's hordes razed low   145
Had vainly labored. As for me, I made
Of my own house beams gallows for myself."

CANTO XIV

Harpy.   *Inferno* XIII, 98

Moved by the pious love of fatherland,
I gathered up the leaf-limbs torn away
And lay them 'neath the wounded plant that was
My fellow-townsman. Then we turned our steps
On to the frontier fixed between the third   5
And second circlets. Here we saw God's wrath
In fearful operation manifest.
A wasteland, reader – for I would make plain
The character of Hell's topography –
Is framed within the dolorous wilderness,   10
In turn encircled by the boiling blood.

We stood, nor dared to cross the boundary,
For past it lay an arid desert, thick
With burning sands like to the Lybian plain
Once trod by noble Cato. Ah, could all   15
Who read but picture what my eyes perceived,
Then were God's vengeance rightly feared on earth!
Weeping forlornly many schools I saw
Of souls, all naked but in divers ways
Suffering their martyrdom, for some supine   20
Lay on the sand, while others, huddled, sat
Immobile and yet others restless strode.
More numerous were those of feverish gait,
And fewest those prostrated but they most
Articulate in pain. On every soul,   25
Descending with an even gentle fall,
Even as mountain snow in windless air,
Rained down dilated flakes of living flame.

As Alexander once beheld his host
Beyond the Indus checked in its advance   30
By flames descending, whence he gave command

To beat the earth clear that the solid fire
Might be extinguished quickly as it fell,
So here the blazing flakes poured ever down
Kindling the sand beneath; the grains were sparks   35
As flint gives under steel. So from beneath
As from above the guilty souls were seared.
Their frenzied hands in ceaseless flickering
Danced over their scorched substance, beating off
The fiery sparks continually renewed.   40

"Lord," I began, "triumphant hitherto
Over all obstacles save for the fiends
Who strove to bar our entrance at the gate,
Who lies there, giant-limbed, with sullen brow
Seeming oblivious of the raining fire,   45
Contorted, while the heat, it would appear,
Distils not his repentance?" Hearing me
Inquire of his state, the figure cried:
"As I was living so I am in death;
Aye, and though Jove exhaust his weary smith,   50
From whom in rage he seized the deathly bolt
To hurl upon me on that fateful day,
And though the forge of Mongibello glow
Through day and night by alternate lackeys fired,
What time he calls 'Help, help, good Vulcan, help' –   55
For so at Phlegra did he whine for aid –
And though his missiles pierce me one by one,
Yet never will I yield and call him lord."
With harsh-toned voice as yet by me unheard
My master answered: "Capaneus, your pride   60
Itself unchecked is your true punishment;
No suffering save such wrath unreconciled
Were just atonement for your insolence."

Then in a milder tone to me he turned:
"One of the Seven, he, who Thebes besieged;   65
God he disdains and still preserves his scorn,
As it appears, nor fears the wrath divine,
Yet, as I bade him mark, his empty spite
Is fit adornment to his impious breast.
Walk after me, be mindful and step not   70
Upon the burning sands, keep your feet well
Within the forest side." No further word
Exchanged, we onward went.
                                  A brooklet ran
Out of the wood, of such a bright blood-red
As still to terrify my memory.   75
As from the Bulicame flows a brook
Shared by the harlots, so this stream across
The desert trickled on its downward course.
The bed and sides were stone and of like sort
The banks; here clearly lay our way ahead.   80
"Since we passed through that portal ever wide
Through which free entrance is denied to none
Not one of all the wonders you have seen
Is worth remark as is this selfsame creek,
Above whose course the flaming hail is quenched."   85
So much my leader volunteered, and I,
Incontinent, urged him at once to slake
The thirst he had aroused. So he went on:
"An olden land under Time's hand decayed,
That men call Crete, lies sea-girt and remote.   90
Once, in the innocence of human dawn,
Her kings held sway. Thereon Mount Ida high
Uprises, murmurous once with leaves and bathed
With purling springs, but desolate now and bare.
This mountain refuge Rhea did elect   95

For her son's cradle and his infant cries
She bade her priests conceal 'neath ritual shouts.
Upright upon this mount an Ancient stands,
Eyes fixed on Rome, as men gaze in a glass
With back to Damiata. Of pure gold   100
His head is formed, all silver arms and breast,
Thence copper to the crotch; his thighs and legs
Are iron, save the hardened clay that shapes
One foot, the right, whereon his weight is leaned.
But for the gold all metals show a flaw   105
Whence issue tears whose flow incessant wears
A passage through the rock, and, trickling down,
In this abyss emerge as Acheron,
Black Styx and Phlegethon. Through this canal
Still downward is their flow until they reach   110
The lowest level of this underworld
And there Cocytus form, whose character
You are to learn." He ceased; I further asked:
"If, as you tell it, this creek is derived
From mortal source, why have our eyes till now   115
Not yet beheld it?" "Hell's abyss," he said,
"Is rounded, and although we now have come
Some distance, ever circling to the left
In spirals toward the centre of the pit,
Yet still the circle we have not fulfilled;   120
Whence, if some novelty perchance appear
It should not be a matter for surprise."
Again I pressed him: "What of Phlegethon
And Lethe? Of the latter you speak not;
The former, though you say it springs from these   125
Infernal waters, yet disclose not where
It flows." "I am content that you should ask
Such questions freely, but the scarlet stream

One answer should supply, while Lethe's shore
Elsewhere you shall behold; its purging flow   130
Affords ablution to the happy souls
Whose penance has unburdened them of guilt.
And now," he added, "we must leave the wood.
See that you follow close behind me here;
The ramps will give us passage; they burn not   135
As does the sand, and over them the air
Is free of blazing hailstones raining down."

CANTO XV

Like dikes the Flemings build against the sea
Between Wissant and Bruges, lest hungry waves
Encroaching flood their towns, or like to those
The Paduans raise on Brenta's lowly banks,
A bulwark for their castles 'gainst the thaws   5
Of Chiarentana's snows, so here – though less
In height and breadth by unknown mason made –
The ramps arose and gave us passage safe,
Protected by the vapors of the stream
From fiery showers and raised above the sand.   10

When we had left the wood so far behind
That looking back I saw no trace of it,
A band of sinners came into our view,
Running beside the ramparts. Each at us
Peered with a narrowed eye, as one who scans   15
A passerby beneath a newborn moon,
With wrinkled brow and penetrating glance.
As we drew near they sharpened still their gaze,
Like an old tailor's fitting thread to eye.
Thus scrutinized intently by the flock   20
One recognized me, seized my robe and cried:
"What miracle is this!" Downward I looked,
Feeling the touch of his extended hand,
And fixed my gaze so keenly on his mien
That through the scorched flesh I knew him again,   25
And reaching down to touch the well-known face
I cried: "O Ser Brunetto, are you here?"
He then: "My son, let it not trouble you
If I, Latini, turn and leave a while
My comrades to their course and walk your way."   30
"Do so, I pray you, do," I conjured him,
"Nay, if you will, I'll stop and sit with you,

If his consent I have who guides me here."
"Alas, my son," he sadly made reply,
"If any of our tribe pause in the race   35
But for a minute, then a hundred years
Under the fire unshielded he must lie.
Therefore proceed; I'll follow at your side
A little while before I join again
My company that mourns its timeless doom."   40

I dared not leave the ramp and match my steps
With his, but walked along with low-bowed head
As one in reverence while he enquired:
"What chance or destiny decrees you come
Down to our world before your days are done,   45
And who is he who guides you on your road?"
"Above, in life serene," I made reply,
"Ere yet my time its middle span had reached,
I stood confused and lost within a vale.
Then he appeared to me, as I turned back –   50
'Twas only yesterday – and leads me home
Over this path." He then rejoined: "If you
But follow faithfully your natal star
You cannot fail of glorious harborage,
So much I knew while yet sweet life endured,   55
And had I not too early come to death
I would have brought you comfort in your toil,
Seeing that Heaven so fully favored you.
Yet still that race of envious ingrates,
Who ages since from Fiésole swooped down,   60
Still marred by crudeness of the mountaineer,
Because of your good works will turn on you;
And meet it is, for hardly should the fig
Bear its sweet fruit among the sour sorbs.

108

Away he turned and with no further word
Across the wasteland scampered with such speed.

Inferno XV, 119–120

Ancient and wide report of this crude folk   65
Brands them as jealous, niggardly and blind;
Divest yourself of every use of theirs.
Such honor does your fate allot to you
That both the parties shall lust for your blood,
But vainly – for the morsel shall be far   70
Beyond the reach of greedy goatish teeth.
Let the Fiesolan beasts turn on themselves,
Refraining from their forays on the plant,
If such may flourish yet among their filth,
In which the Roman seed may thrive again   75
That still remained what time the nest was made
Of so much malice." Here he ceased and I:
"Had my prayers been fulfilled you would not yet
Be banished from the world of humankind,
For in my mind is fixed – and moves me now –   80
Your dear and kind paternal image when
Up in the living world from day to day
You taught me how men live beyond their time,
And while I live the gratitude I feel
Must and will find expression in my words.   85
What you relate of trials yet to come
I shall transcribe and gloss against a text
Yet to be read me, if so far I rise,
By an all-knowing lady. Come what may,
So only that my conscience gnaw me not,   90
Against ill fate I am full fortified.
Your earnest comes not newly to my ears;
I am content: let Fortune spin her wheel,
The ploughman wield his mattock as he will."
Here, backward glancing over his right cheek,   95
My master eyed me, adding his assent:
"He listens well who notes the lesson down."

109

Of Ser Brunetto as we walked along,
I asked of his companions, who might be
The well-known or the greatest. He replied,   100
"My time were short to tell you of them all;
Some names you may well learn, of others best
It will be to say naught. All here, in brief,
Were men of letters, clerics and renowned,
And all in life stained with the selfsame sin.   105
Yonder runs Priscian with the sorry pack,
And Francis of Accorso; if you had
A longing to behold such scurviness
You might have sight of him whose seat was moved
By papal edict from the Arno shore   110
To Bacchiglione's, where he laid to rest
His nerves distended by their evil use.
More would I cite but longer may I not
Converse nor walk beside you; from the sand
I see new smoke arise: a company   115
I must not join approaches. Only this
I ask of you: my *Treasure* keep in mind
In which I yet live on – and so, farewell."

Away he turned and with no further word
Across the wasteland scampered with such speed   120
As to seem one who runs Verona's course
For the green pallium, nay, such was his stride
As would become the winner in that race.

CANTO XVI

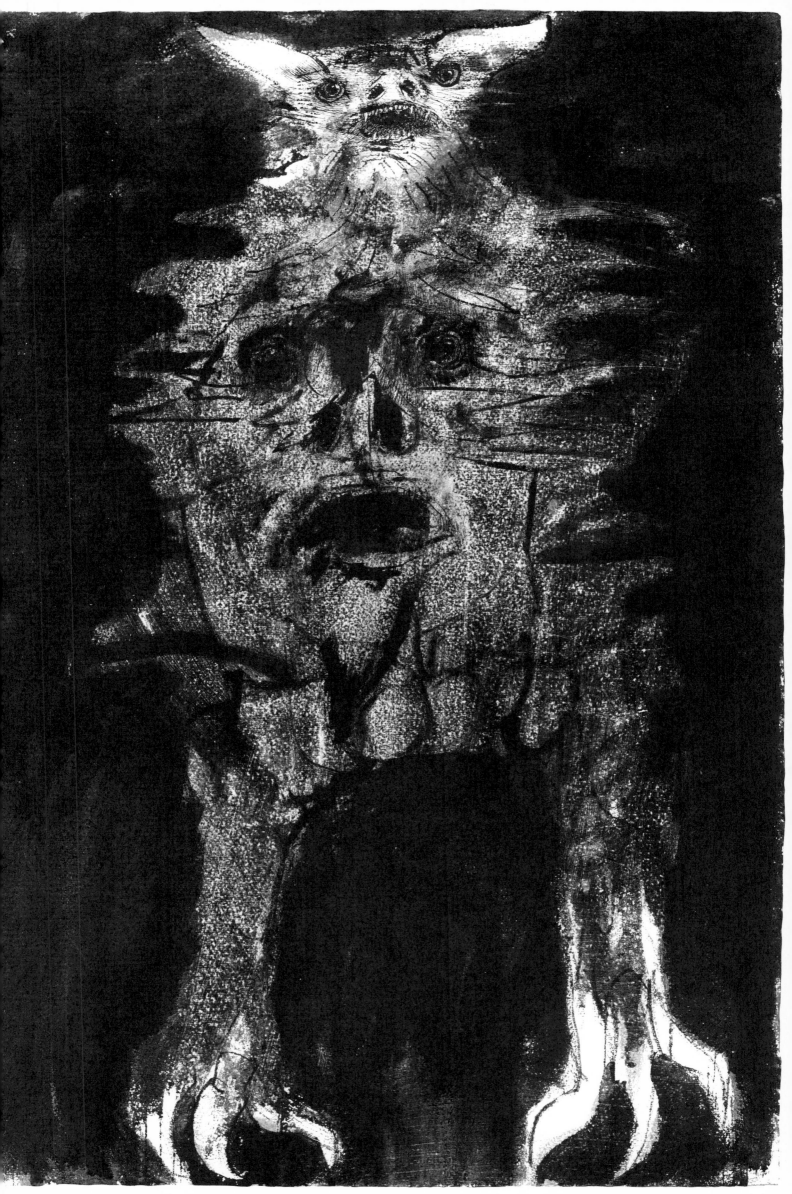

The Violent against Nature.   *Inferno* XVI

Already had we come to where we heard
The distant roar of waters pouring down
In the successive circle, not unlike
The humming in a hive of honey bees,
When three shades all at once detached themselves   5
From out a company that swept by us
Under the biting downpour of the flames.
They came to us a-running; crying out,
"You there, whose costume shows you to be one
Of our ill country, stay your steps awhile!"   10
Alas, what countless old and fresh-made scars
I saw upon them burnt in by the fire;
It hurts me still to think upon the sight.
My master was not heedless of their cries
But turned to me and said: "Await them now;   15
To such as these your courtesy is due,
And were it not for darting down of fire,
Which is the nature of this place, I'd say
That haste were more befitting you than them."
As we stood still their ancient wail of woe   20
They started up again, and reaching us
All three clasped hands and made themselves a wheel.
And as the wont of wrestlers was of old
Who naked and anointed for the ring
Would, sparring, seek for holds and vantages   25
Before they fell to trading thrusts and blows,
So here they wheeled and each one fixed his face
Upon me so that ever neck and feet
Travelled a course contrary each to each.

"If the grim squalor of this sandy spot   30
Arouses scorn for us and our petition" –
So one began – "and our stained, burnt appearance,

113

May our good reputations move your spirit
To tell us who you are, whose living feet
Press on through Hell in such security.   35
This one, upon whose tracks you see me tread,
Though he go naked and despoiled of hair
Was of a higher rank than you believe,
For he was grandson to the good Gualdrada.
Guido Guerra was his name and in his life   40
With wit and sword he mightily achieved.
And coming after me, grinding the sand,
Is Tegghiaio Aldobrandi, he whose voice
Should have been welcomed in the world above.
And I, thus put upon the cross with them,   45
Am Jácopo Rusticucci; beyond doubt
More than aught else my cruel wife does me ill."
If I had had protection from the fire
I'd have jumped down to join them on the sand
And I believe my sage would have allowed it.   50
But, as I should have burnt and scorched myself,
Fear conquered, overcoming my good will
Which made me avid to embrace them all.
Then I began: "Nay, not contempt but sorrow
Your sad condition fixed in me, so deep   55
As to long linger ere it be effaced,
Soon as my master here addressed to me
The words whereby I understood that such
Folk as you are were coming toward us.
I am your fellow townsman; and all my life   60
In loving recollection I have heard
Of your fair deeds and honorable names.
I leave the gall and go to the sweet fruits
That my true leader promised me, but first
I must descend down to the very center."   65

114

"So may for many years your soul escort
Your members," so the same spirit replied,
"And so your fame leave lustre after you,
Tell us, do courtesy and worth yet dwell
Within our city as was once their wont,   70
Or have they utterly abandoned it?
Guglielmo Borsiere, newly come to share
Our anguish (yonder goes he with his mates),
Sorely distresses us with his report."
"New folk and profits made too easily   75
In thee, O Florence, have engendered pride
And lack of measure, whence your tears now flow."
So I apostrophized with face upraised.
The trio, taking such words for their answer,
Eyed each his mates, as men who hear truth spoken,   80
Then answered, "If at other times it costs you
So little to content your hearers, then
You are most blessed in aptitude of speech.
And if from these drab regions you emerge
And once more look upon the shining stars   85
When you are pleased to say 'once I was there'
Take care to speak of us to those above."

So quickly that one hardly could have uttered
An *amen*, they all disappeared from sight.
Whereat my master too chose to move on.   90
I followed him and we had not gone far
Before the sound of water came so near
That we could scarce have heard each other's voice.
Just as that stream that follows its own course
From Monte Veso downward toward the East   95
Along the left side of the Apennines
(Called Acquacheta in its upper branch,

115

Leaving that name behind it at Forlì)
Reverberates above San Benedetto,
Through one descent alone downfalling, where   100
A thousand should receive it – even so
Down from a rocky wall precipitate
We came upon a dark cascade, so thund'ring
That in brief time it would have bruised our ears.

I wore a cord that girded me around   105
And with it I had thought one time to snare
The leopard with the brightly spotted pelt.
Now here, obedient to my captain's wish,
I loosed it from me, passing it to him
All looped and convoluted in a ball.   110
He, turning to the right and leaning out
Beyond the brink, then cast it far below
Into the chasm. "Some new thing," I said
Within myself, "must answer this new sign
My master follows closely with his eye."   115
Ah, how much caution must we learn to use
In company with those who can perceive
Not only deeds but our most inward thoughts!
He said to me: "Soon will he now ascend
Whom I expect and whom your thought conceives;   120
Soon will he be discovered to your eye."
Ever before the truth that bears the semblance
Of falsehood must a man restrain his lips,
For even though blameless he incurs reproach.
But here I must speak out and by the notes   125
Of this my Comedy and by my hope
They may not fail to win your lasting favor,
O reader, I will swear I saw approach
Upswimming through that dark and heavy air

116

A shape of marvel to the firmest heart. 130
It moved as one who, having dived to free
An anchor grappled on a reef or fouled
By some sea obstacle, comes up again
With arms outstretched and nether limbs withdrawn.

CANTO XVII

"Behold the monster of the venomed tail:
No armor, no walled ramparts may withstand
Its malice, nor high mountains check its march;
Its fetid breath pollutes the living world."
Thus Virgil in my ear and as he spoke   5
Beckoned the beast to anchor on the stone
Whereon we stood that rimmed the yawning gulf.
Obedient, the image of foul fraud
Approached and beached its head and upper half,
Leaving the tail suspended in the void.   10
The face the hideous hybrid turned toward us
Was of a just man, kindly and benign;
The subjoined body was of serpent shape.
Two arms projected, hairy to the pits;
Breast, flanks and back with brilliant arabesques   15
Were all embroidered and in vivid hues
Were overlaid gay whorls and cunning knots
So subtly traced no Turk or Tartar yet
Their like has woven nor Arachne's skill
Had e'er conceived such richness of design.   20

As skiffs rest sometimes idle on the bank
Half in the water and half dry on shore,
Or as the beaver sets himself to fish
By Northern streams where guzzling Germans dwell,
In like position did the beast draw up   25
On the stone margin that contains the sand;
Wide o'er the chasm flickered the forked tail,
Envenomed, like a scorpion's, keen to strike.
The poet spoke, "Now must we turn aside
A little and approach the evil beast   30
Couched to await us." Rightward then we veered
A full ten steps to leave a goodly space
Between us and the desert with its flames.

As we drew nearer to the creature's side
I saw yet further on upon the sand   35
More figures seated almost on the brink.
My master counseled: "Go, survey their state
And make complete your knowledge of this ring
But let your speech with yonder folk be short.
I will engage meanwhile this grotesque beast   40
To lend his wings and back for our descent."
Along the seventh circle's outer edge
I made my way alone. The guilty here
Sat all disconsolate, their agony
Streaming from out their eyes; now here now there   45
Their restless hands moved, slapping off the sparks
That pelted down or blistered on the ground.
Dogs in the summer heat they brought to mind
Who paw and muzzle agitate against
The bites of fleas or flies or other pests.   50
Closely I scanned their features seared by fire
And none I knew, but noted how on each
A money-bag hung pendant from the neck,
Each with its own tint and its own device
And each devoured by its owner's eyes.   55
The first I marked showed on a field of gold
An azure lion, while his neighbor's purse
Displayed a goose, cream white, on blood-red ground.
Then one whose white bag bore a fat blue sow
Hailed me: "What business brings you to this ditch?   60
Move on. And, since you yet are living man,
Know that my fellow townsman who still breathes,
Vitaliano, has his place reserved
And is to join us, sitting on my left.
Sole Paduan I among these Florentines   65
Who trumpet in my ear their endless cry:

122

And none I knew, but noted how on each
A money-bag hung pendant from the neck.

Inferno XVII, 52–53

'Soon comes he, sovereign cavalier of all,
Bearing the three black ramsheads on his pouch.' "
So saying he distorted his great mouth
Protruding his great tongue as an ox does,   70
Licking its nose. I fearing to annoy
Him who had bidden me to linger not
Turned me away from those prostrated souls.

My guide, I found, already sat astride
The monster's back. Exhorting me he spoke: 75
"Mount boldly now and put aside all fear:
Stout heart is needed for this strange descent.
Sit here before me. I will be your shield
Lest the envenomed tail might do you harm."
As one so shaken by a fever bout   80
That but to look at shade he shivers, chilled,
With nails left pallid by retreating blood,
So I became at this admonishment.
Shame only gave me strength, for shame it is
That makes the vassal brave in his lord's sight;   85
Upon those dreadful shoulders up I climbed
And "Hold me tight" I thought to say but voice
I found not as I would. However he
Whose aid at other perils had not failed
Failed me not here. He clasped me in his arms   90
And cried: "Now, Geryon, on, and ply your wings
In circles slow and gentle downward flight;
Be mindful of the mortal weight you bear."
Then, as a galley slowly slips from port,
Stern foremost, so it glided from the bank   95
And once in open space, turned on itself
Head pointed where the tail had stood. Eel-like
It moved its head and with its shaggy arms
Drew in the air as swimmers grasp the sea.

123

Never was known a panic like to mine,   100
I do believe, not even when the reins
Dropped from the hands of Phaethon while his car
Veered from its track and scorched the vault of heaven,
Nor when poor Icarus felt his waxen wings
Melt from his shoulders while his father's cry,   105
"Ah woeful flight," rang on his frightened ears.

Suspended helpless in the empty air
I found myself, and in the engulfing dark
Save for the beast who bore us nought I saw.
Down, slowly down, with smooth slow wheels he moved 110
Yet only air up-rushing on my face
Betrayed our motion. To the right I heard
Far, far below the crashing cataract.
I leaned down then and bent my head to look –
And gripped the tighter to my saddle. Flames   115
Beneath me glowed; wild cries assailed my ear
And trembling I held grimly to my seat
Beginning then to see what earlier
I could not: how we spiraled ever down,
For sights of horror ever nearer came   120
And changed direction to my frightened gaze.
And as a falcon, long aloft in vain
And sighting neither lure nor feathered prey,
Exhausted seeks the earth whence he arose
Light winged and eager (while the fowler cries,   125
"So down you come, alas") and, ruffled, sulks
Standing some distance from his master's side,
In such a fashion Geryon set us down
In the deep well close by the sheer rock wall,
And having freed his shoulders of our weight   130
Shot off at once, like whistling bolt from bow.

124

CANTO XVIII

A place in Hell there is called Evilpits,
Hewn out of iron-dark stone like to the cliffs
That hem it in, and in its heart a well
Yawns wide and deep. Of this in proper place
I shall say more. The strip between the well   5
And high enclosing rocky walls is round
And corrugated by ten dismal troughs.
Picture a castle's walls protected by
Successive moats; such was the figure here,
And, as across them, bridges might be thrown   10
So here did craggy causeways link like spokes,
Reaching from outer edge to inner pit,
The pouches with their ridges high between.

'T was here that Geryon shook us from his back;
Leftward the poet turned and I behind,   15
And on my right new horrors met my eye.
Torments as yet unseen and new tormenters
Packed the first trench. Naked the sinners moved
In double file, one from the center out
Faced toward us while the inner line moved on   20
As we were walking but with hastier stride.
Even so the Romans, for the mighty press
Of pilgrims, in the year of jubilee
Devised a scheme for traffic of the throng,
On one side sending those whose steps are turned   25
Up toward the castle and St. Peter's shrine,
Directing in the other lane the folk
Who cross the Tiber, making toward the mount.
Both columns as they trudged on the bleak stone
Were lashed by hornèd demons, plying fast   30
Their heavy scourges as they walked behind.
How briskly did the culprits lift their heels

Under the curling lash; none stood to wait
The second blow!
             My glance, as I walked by,
Fell on one rogue thus flogged and I cried out: 35
"Thirst of his sight my eyes have slaked ere now."
As recollection came I stayed my step
And my kind captain stopped and gave consent
That I might somewhat of our path retrace.
The beaten rogue by lowering of his brow   40
Sought to conceal himself but sought in vain.
I called out: "You there, bending down your glance,
Unless you bear false features, well I know,
Caccianemico. What brings you to stew
In such a sauce?" "Unwillingly," he said,   45
"I give you answer, but your open speech,
Recalling to my mind the world of old,
Compels my utterance. I it was who led
My sister to obey the lustful will
Of the marchese, though the scabrous tale   50
May be amongst the living elsewise told.
Nor am I here the only Bolognese,
Nay, rather in such plenty we abound
That scarce so many tongues 'sipa' pronounce
Twixt Sávena and Reno. For the proof   55
It will suffice you but to call to mind
Our avaricious temper." As he spoke
A demon dealt him out a mighty clip
And shouted: "Move on, pimp, no women here
For coinage!" Then my escort I rejoined   60
And but a few steps further on we neared
A crag projecting from the inner banks;
Climbing hereon we rightward turned our steps
Across its granite back and left behind
The outer wheeling circle of the damned.   65

128

We mounted on the arch that rises high
Allowing passage to the beaten files
And Virgil spoke: "Halt here and let the sight
Confront you of the inner sinful ring
Who, walking as we did, did not reveal   70
Their faces to us." From the bridge we scanned
The second file that circled counterwise
To those we'd seen but suffered like distress.
Without my prompting my good master said:
"Behold that mighty one who treads his path   75
Seeming to shed no tear for all his hurt;
How much of royal aspect he retains!
For he is Jason, whose stout heart and wit
Beguiled the Colchians of their Golden Fleece;
Lemnos he visited, what time that isle   80
Only by harsh and heartless womankind
Was peopled; they themselves their men had slain.
There he with amorous gestures and fair words
Falsely betrayed the maid Hypsipyle,
Betrayer of her sex. Then sailing off   85
He left her all alone and great with child.
For such offense he pays forever here,
And vengeance for Medea too is wrought.
All of like guilt share in his punishment.
Enough you know now of the first grim pouch   90
And those who writhe and shudder in its hold."

Now had we come to where the narrow span
Crosses the second ridge and therefrom springs
To form a second arch. From the next cleft
We heard a whinnying sound of snorting snouts   95
And scraping hands. A crust of slimy mold
Covered the walls, by exhalations formed

129

In foulness steaming up from far below,
Disgusting to the eye and nose alike.
So dark the bottom lay beyond our sight   100
That only when we stood atop the span
Could we discern it. Here we made our way
And peering down we saw souls deep submerged
In filthy dung, as human privies yield.
Throwing my glance yet deeper I could see   105
A head so dark beshitten as to hide
If he were clerk or layman. Loud he yelled:
"Why fix your hungry stare on me alone
Among so many thus befouled?" "Because,"
I made reply, "if memory fail me not,   110
We two have met before and I knew you
Alessio of Lucca, although then your locks
Were not so sodden." Then he cried again,
Beating his pumpkin head, "The honeyed words
Of fawning flattery my lips poured forth   115
Have earned for me my station in this spot."
"Now further lean," I heard my leader say,
"So that your eye may fix upon the face
Of that disheveled, squalid harridan,
Now standing, now a-squat and never still   120
But always scratching with her dung-filled nails;
She is Thaïs, the harlot, who replied
When her fond lover asked: 'What thanks have I?'
'Beyond all measure.' . . . Now let us begone
With satiated sight of this foul scene."   125

But always scratching with her dung-filled nails;
She is Thaïs, the harlot.

Inferno XVIII, 121–122

CANTO XIX

O Simon Magus with your sorry school,
You whose rapacity adulterates
With silver and with gold the things of God
That should with virtue only be espoused,
Now let the trumpet sound a blast for you   5
Since to the third pouch is your ilk assigned.

Already we had climbed above the tomb
Next to the flatterers' trench and on mid arch
We stood that dominates the central ditch.
Wisdom Supreme, how wondrous is thy art   10
In Heaven and Earth revealed and in the world
Of evil, and how just are thy decrees!
Along the sides and on the valley floor
I saw the livid stone all perforate
With pits all round and all of equal size.   15
No less in width nor wider did they seem
Than the compartments for the christening priests
Within my own fair San Giovanni where
Not many years ago I broke one wide
To save a babe that would have drowned therein,   20
(And may this serve to seal the slanderous tongues).
Projecting from the mouth of every hole
A sinner's feet and nether legs appeared
Down to the calf, the rest was thrust within.
Each pair of soles was bathed in lambent flames   25
Which kept the joints a-twitching with such force
As would have burst asunder ropes or withes.
As flames play o'er a surface spread with oil
So here they licked the skin from heel to toe.
"Say, Master, who is he that shows his grief,   30
More wildly kicking than his suffering mates
And feeds a hungrier and darker flame?"

133

He answered: "If you will I'll bear you down
Across the lower rim that deeper slopes
That from his own lips you may hear his wrongs."   35
And I rejoined: "Your pleasure is my joy;
You are my lord and know that my desire
Swerves not from your will and you know as well
What here I leave unsaid." On the fourth ridge
We turned and, leftward bearing, clambered down   40
Into the narrow bottom, pierced with holes.
My gentle guide did not release his grasp
Nor set me down until we stood before
The tomb of him who stirred his plaintive shank.
"You there, with upper half reversed below,   45
Earth-planted like a pole, who e'er you be,
O wretched soul, speak out, if speak you may."
(I spoke and stood above him as the friar
Stands o'er the pit where the assassin bound
Has called him back to win delay of death.)   50
He cried out: "Boniface, 'tis you, 'tis you
Who stand erect above. By some few years
Prevision has deceived me. So soon then
You've satisfied your avarice for loot
For love of which you scrupled not to trick   55
The fairest lady nor to do her ill!"
His words left me bewildered, like to one
Made game of by a frivolous reply
And I stood speechless. Virgil quickly said:
"Tell him at once 'I am not who you think.'"   60
And as he bade me so I answer made.
Whereat the spirit's heels in frenzy writhed
And then in plaintive accents charged with sighs
He groaned: "Well then, what would you have of me?
If but to learn of my identity   65

134

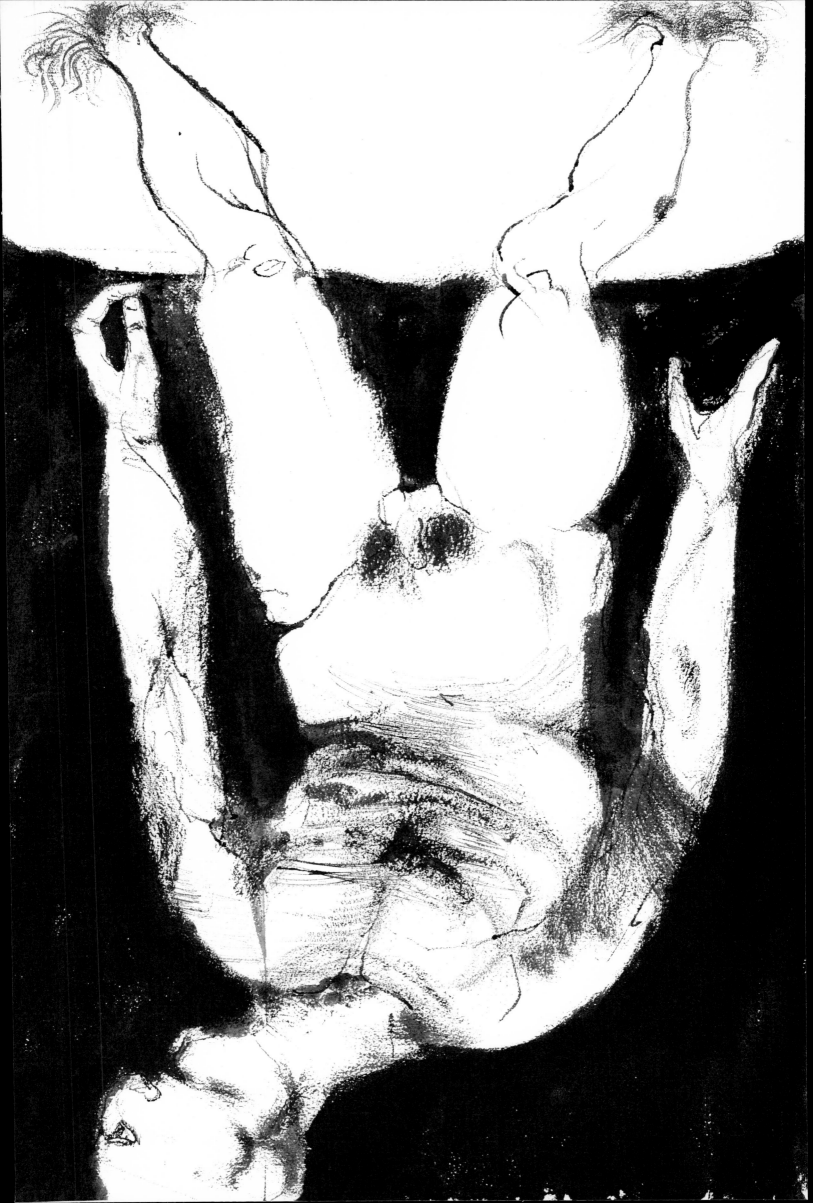

Projecting from the mouth of every hole
A sinner's feet and nether legs appeared
Down to the calf, the rest was thrust within.

Inferno XIX, 22–24

You undertook this arduous descent,
Learn that the papal mantle once I bore
And was a faithful son to the She-bear,
So zealous to enrich her brood of cubs
That up on earth I pocketed much wealth   70
And here in Hell myself. Below my head
Down through the narrow fissure of this rock
Those who preceded me in simony
Lie each on each and down I too will slip
When I must yield my place to him I thought   75
Your voice betrayed when first I questioned you;
Yet for a longer time I thus reversed
Have lain and toasted, kicking heel and toe,
Than he will stay atop with sizzling sole,
For hot on him another will descend   80
Of evil works, a shepherd without law
From out the west, and cover up us both.
A modern Jason like to him we see
In Maccabees, and as the first was weak
Before his king so will the new one bend   85
Complaisant to the regnant prince of France."
I know not here if I too rashly spoke,
Yet I could not refrain and challenged him:
"Tell me now, pray, what fee our Lord required
Of Peter when He handed him the keys?   90
Surely no more he asked than 'Follow me.'
Nor gold and silver Peter and the rest
Took from Matthias when to him was given
The place left vacant by the guilty soul.
So you have justly earned your punishment;   95
Stay planted, counting your ill-gotten gains
Which made you bold and free to challenge Charles,
And were it not for reverence of the keys

135

That once were yours in mortal life above
I would speak out in heavier reproof,   100
For all the world is saddened by your greed,
Oppressing good men and exalting knaves.
Aye, shepherd, 'twas of you and of your like
The Evangelist had foreknowledge when he saw
The whore upon the waters wantoning   105
With kings, the same that had been born of old
With seven heads and from ten horns drew strength
So long as right and virtue pleased her spouse.
Priests who have made a god of brazen gold,
Say how you differ from idolators   110
Save that you worship hundreds, they but one?
Ah Constantine, what evil seed was sown
Not by your true conversion but the gift
Which the first wealthy father took from thee!"
Helpless he listened to my stinging lay   115
While under spur of anger or remorse
His feet moved faster in their futile dance.
My leader heard me out in full content,
As I could see, pleased by my truthful words.
Wherefore with both his arms he took me up   120
And holding me tight clasped against his breast
He climbed again the way of our descent,
Nor wearied of the burden that he bore
But carried me up to the bridge's crest
That crosses from the fourth verge to the fifth.   125
Here very gently did he set me down
Upon the steep and broken face of rock
Where even goats might find the going rough.
And here another valley lay exposed.

CANTO XX

New anguish gives me matter for my verse
In this the twentieth canto of the first
Great canticle, that treats of the submerged.
I had disposed my every eager sense
To contemplate the plain revealed to me,   5
Laved as it was by tears of tortured shades.
So in the sad ravine my eyes made out
A slowly wending file of silent folk
Weeping and plodding with a heavy stride
As chanting pilgrims march in this our world.   10
As my glance travelled downward from their heads,
Each one, I saw, was twisted all awry
In wondrous wise betwixt the neck and chest.
Each face was turned about to front the loins
And so distorted all must backward walk   15
Having no power to see the road ahead.
Paralysis, it may be, here on earth
Has wrought such shape on some, but for my part
I cannot think so, none such have I seen.
Bethink yourself, O Reader, as you hope   20
That God may grant you profit of this text,
How vainly might I strive to check my grief
When I beheld our common human form
Disfigured so the ever-flowing tears
Poured down the channel where the buttocks join.   25
I wept indeed and leaned my sob-racked frame
Against a jutting rock. My escort spoke:
"Are you then still like all the other fools?
Here pity lives that properly were dead.
What greater wickedness is there than his   30
Who views God's justice with a vain regret?
Come lift your head, see him for whom the earth
Gaped wide while all Thebes witnessed and cried out,

'Amphiaraus, look where you leap; say why
Do you desert the battle?' But he fell   35
Headlong to Minos, who detains all souls.
Note that his shoulders are become his breast;
Because he strove to see too far ahead
He now looks back and heel-first bends his step.
Mark there Tiresias, who marvellous change   40
Suffered from maleness to the female form
And had to bide his time and strike again
The serpents intertwined ere he regained
His manlike mold. Back-treading on his paunch
Aruns comes next, whose cavern home was high   45
Carved in the white Carrara, on the hills
Whose leafy stillness only woodsmen know.
From this fair prospect he could contemplate
Unhindered the bright stars and distant sea.
She, coming close behind, whom you see not,   50
Shielding her bosom and her flowing hair
From our sight hidden, she is Manto's shade
Whose wandering quest for weary years endured
Till in my native town she came to rest.
Touching on this, I'd have you listen further: 55
After her father had departed life
And Bacchus' city had become enslaved,
She wandered through the world for many years.
Above us, in fair Italy, lies a lake
Under the hills enclosing Germany,   60
High in the Tyrol; it is called Benacus.
More than a thousand springs, I think, whose source
Is in these quiet waters, bathe the Apennines,
Sloping from Garda to Camonica.
Right in the middle lies a place where Trent's   65
Shepherd and those of Brescia and Verona

140

Mark there Tiresias.   *Inferno* xx, 40

Could give their blessings, if they went that way.
Peschiera, fair and rugged fortress, rises
Apt to withstand Brescians and Bergamasks
Where the surrounding shore comes lowest down;   70
There all that Garda's womb may not contain
Must of necessity descend; it forms
A river, flowing southward through green fields.
Soon as its course begins, men call this water
Benacus no longer, it is Mincio now   75
As far as Governo where it joins the Po.
It runs not long before it finds a plain
Which it spreads over, making thus a marsh
That oft is noisome in the summer season.
Here was it that the cruel maiden, passing,   80
Saw firm land in the middle of the swamp,
Untilled and empty of inhabitants.
There, to escape all human fellowship
She stayed with all her train to ply her arts,
There lived her days, there left her lifeless flesh.   85
Afterwards men who dwelt in those environs
Collected in that place which, as the swamp
Encircled it, gave natural defense.
They built their city over those dead bones
And for her sake who settled first the place,   90
Drawing no further lot, they called it Mantua.
Time was the folk within were more in number
Ere Casalodi's folly had acceded
To the false stratagem of Pinamonte.
I set you right in case you ever hear   95
Another story of my town's beginnings,
So that no falsehood may defraud the truth."
I answered him: "My master, your account
Beyond all question wins in me such credence

That other stories would be burnt out coals. 100
But tell me of the souls that pass before us
If you see any worthy of remark:
To that concern my mind always reverts."
Then said he: "Yonder shade, with beard projecting
Out from his cheek upon his dark-hued shoulders, 105
Was augur at the time when Greece was stripped
Of males so that scarce any had remained
Even in the cradles: he with Calchas set
In Aulis the hour to cut the mooring ropes.
Euripilus was his name and in one passage 110
My lofty tragedy so sings of him, as you
Must know, for you well know it through and through.
The other one, so slender in the flanks,
Is Michael Scot; in very truth he knew
The game of sorcery and its deceptions. 115
Guido Bonatti, see: mark there Asdente,
Now would he gladly have concerned himself
With hide and cord, but late comes his repentance.
Look at the sorry women who put aside
Needle and spool and thread to follow witchcraft, 120
Working their spells with images and herbs.
But come away; by now Cain with his thorns
Stands on the frontier of the hemispheres,
Brushing the ocean wave below Seville,
And last night's moon already waxed full round 125
As you should well remember, for it did you
At no time any harm in the deep wood."

Such were his words and as he spoke we moved.

CANTO XXI

Thus, touching on such things as lie beyond
The scope of this my Comedy, we passed
From rocky bridge to bridge, and on the crest
We paused to look upon another slot
Of Evilpits, with futile plaints replete   5
And to my eye most marvellously dark.
As when Venetians in their Arsenal
In winter season boil their sticky pitch
While stormy weather keeps their ships ashore,
And some construct new hulls and some recaulk   10
The ribs of galleys that have voyaged far;
Some hammer on the prow, some at the poop,
And some make oars while others splice their ropes,
Still others patch the mainsail or the jib;
So here, warmed not by fire but by God's art,   15
Within the fissure steamed a viscid stuff
That clung fast to the bank on either hand.

The pitch I saw, but could mark naught within
Save only bubbles that the boiling made
As the whole cauldron rose and fell compressed.   20
While I was peering down with eye intent
My leader, calling to me, "Look, look here!"
Drew me to take my station at his side.
Then did I turn as one who longs to see
What he must flee from yet whom sudden fear   25
Dismays so that he lingers not to look.
And back of us I saw a devil come,
All black and running up the craggy bank
With outstretched wing and fleet upon his feet.
Ah, how ferocious was his evil grin!   30
What cruel nature did his acts betray!
His high and pointed shoulder bore aloft

A straddled sinner's haunches, while the fiend
With either hand clutched fast the sinewed calf.
"O Badpaws", he cried, standing on our bridge,   35
"Here comes one of Saint Zita's senators.
You heave him in while I go back for more;
I've found a spot where these fat rascals swarm.
Save for Bonturo all are grafters there
And 'yes' for 'no' they gladly change for cash!"   40
He spoke and hurled the hapless victim in
And hastened up the bank again; no hound
Unleashed to set on thief more swiftly sprang.
The sinner plunged and re-emerged convulsed;
The demons who had cover of the bridge   45
Cried out, "The Holy Face is no help here;
Our sinners somewhat differently disport
Themselves from those in Serchio. If our hooks
You do not fancy, keep below the pitch."
Then, gouging him with a full score and more   50
Of barbs, they cried again: "Here play your games
Beneath the surface; learn to hide your frauds."
They used their prongs as scullions ply the fork
Under the cook's surveillance to assure
The meat be roundly boiled within the pot.   55
My master then: "So that it may not seem
That you are with me, squat behind a rock
For safe concealment, and, whate'er affront
Be offered me, fear not. Their trafficking
I know of old; I can cope with their shifts."   60

So speaking he crossed over the bridge head,
Reaching the sixth embankment where he had
Full need of all the boldness he displayed.
With that tempestuous fury of curs roused

146

The sinner plunged and re-emerged convulsed.

Inferno XXI, 44

To set upon the beggar at the gate   65
Who needs must stop and plead from where he stands,
The fiends rushed fiercely forth from 'neath the bridge
With hooks upraised against him. He cried out:
"Let none of you attack me. Put aside
Your barbs and let your chief attend my words;   70
And after think to slice me, if you dare."
As with one voice they cried: "Badtail, come forth!"
And held themselves in check while one stepped out
Approaching Virgil, grumbling as he came,
"Small good 'twill do him." But my guide replied: 75
"Think you then, Badtail, I have so far fared
Secure 'gainst every subterfuge of Hell
Without propitious fate and grace divine?
Make way for us since Heaven's decree it is
That I must lead the way through this wild wood."   80
Dismayed, the insolent imp let fall his fork,
Charging his company: "Leave him untouched."
Whereat my master raised his voice and called:
"Come now in safety to me, you who sit
A-squat behind the cover of the bridge."   85
So out I came and ran to my lord's side,
And all the devils started forth toward me,
Then panic seized me lest they break their pact.
Mistrustful was I as the men-at-arms
I saw long years ago 'neath pledge of truce   90
Depart Caprona's walls 'twixt files of foes.

I ranged myself as closely as I might
Beside the poet, daring not to turn
My eyes from their grim aspect boding ill.
With lowered hook one muttered to his mate: 95
"What say you, shall we nick him on the rump?"

147

– "Aye, tickle him." The master devil wheeled
From parley with my leader, snarling out:
"Peace, Bristlepate, be still, be still!" then turned
Again, addressing us: "Upon this crag   100
No further may you go, for the sixth arch
Has crumbled and lies broken at the base.
If further progress be your purpose fixed,
Pursue this grotto's bridle-path awhile
Until you meet another bridge, intact.   105
But yesterday, five hours past the time
We speak today, did mark twelve hundred years
And sixty-six since shattering of this bridge.
I will send with you some few lads of mine
To spy if any sinner show himself.   110
Proceed with them; they will not misbehave.
Come forward, Harlequin, and Frostfoot too" –
So he began the roll – "and you, Dogsnout,
And Curlybeard, come forth and take command,
Let Dragonscowl and Libbycock fall in;   115
Scratchdog and sharp-toothed Tusker, come along,
With Farfarel and madman Ruddyface.
Watch out for rascals bubbling in the tar
And see that these two reach the next outcrop
Of jutting rock that crosses all the pits."   120

"Oh master," I protested, "what a sight
Confronts me! Let us rather go alone
Since you well know the way. No need have we
Of escort, surely I would ask for none.
If you are not less keen-eyed than your wont   125
How can you fail to see them gnash their teeth
And threaten mischief with their baleful stares?"
And he to me: "I will not have you fear;

Let them bare dripping fangs to their content,
'Tis only boiling sinnermeat they crave." 130
On the left bank the whole platoon then wheeled,
Each imp with tongue outthrust as in salute
To their appointed chief; he made reply,
Emitting from his arse a bugle blast.

CANTO XXII

I have seen troops of horsemen in my day
Break camp, and hold reviews and ranks deploy
For the attack, and sometimes in retreat
Retire discomfited; vedettes I've seen
Reconnoitring your country, Aretines;   5
I've witnessed cavalcades and tournaments
And knightly jousts. The martial signals given
Were sometimes trumpet calls and sometimes bells
Or drums or beacons from a castle tower –
I thought all kinds of war alarms I knew,   10
Our own or alien, but never yet
Had I heard such exotic style of horn
To set in motion horse or infantry
Or galley scanning land and stars for signs.

So with the demons ten we marched along,   15
Dread company – but "in the church consort
With saints and with good topers at the inn."
The boiling pitch I eyed continually
To study every aspect of this pouch
And learn the state of such as blistered here.   20
And just as dolphins, when they indicate
To sailors by the arching of their backs
That they should hasten to make safe their ships,
So here from time to time a sinner flashed
Out of the steaming broth to win relief,   25
And quick as lightning plunged below again.
And, as along the limits of a pool
Frogs range themselves with only snout exposed,
Likewise the wretches lined the banks to breathe
But dived back quickly in the deeper pitch   30
As Curlybeard and his platoon approached.
But, as it happens sometimes that one frog

Unwary lingers while his fellows jump,
So here I saw – and shudder to recall
The sight – one rogue too tardy in his spring.   35
Scratchdog, close by, lunged fiercely with his fork
And grappling him by his tar-tangled locks
Hauled him ashore; the luckless captive stood
Before us, black and dripping like an otter.
(I knew by now the name of every imp   40
For I had listened when the roll was called
And heeded as they spoke among themselves.)
Baying in chorus they yelped: "Ruddyface,
Use claws and rip him up; let's have his hide!"
I whispered: "Master, if you may, pray learn   45
Who is this creature helpless in the clutch
Of cruel foes." My guide approached the knave,
Enquiring whence he came and he replied:
"My birth was in the Kingdom of Navarre;
My sire a wastrel and a suicide,   50
My mother sent me forth to serve a lord.
Thence good King Thibault's liegeman I became
And in his court such dealing I devised
For which I give accounting in this broth."
Then Tusker, rightly called, for from his mouth 55
Two gleaming tusks emerged as from a boar's,
Let the poor rascal taste their cutting edge.
Cruel cats had cornered the defenseless mouse!
However, Curlybeard threw covering arms
About him, snarling: "Stand aside while I   60
Enfork him." Turning then he bade my chief:
"Ask more of him if more you wish to hear
Before these fellows tear him limb from limb."
Promptly said Virgil: "Tell us, in your band
Of villains lurking underneath the pitch   65

154

Lies there another Latin?" "Why, just now
I left behind one of a neighboring land;
Would I were still protected as he is
And out of reach of claws and grappling hooks."
"Too long we've waited" – this from Libbycock,   70
Who, as he spoke, lunged with his lance and pruned
A goodly fragment of the captive's arm.
Then Dragonscowl snapped at his tender calves,
Whereat their provost cast a glance around,
Resentful. When a devil's peace was made   75
My captain spoke again and quickly asked:
"Whose comradeship was his that you recall
Regretfully now you have come ashore?"
"Brother Gomita of Gallura 'twas,"
He answered, "vessel of all trickery.   80
His master's foes he held within his grasp
And dealt so with them that each gave him praise;
He took their coin and let them go in peace.
So much he boasts; in this and other deals
He proved himself the very prince of cheats.   85
Beside him Michael Zanche has his post,
From Logodoro he; their tireless tongues
Tell ever of Sardina and its folk.
I would say more but look how yonder fiend
Bares wolfish fangs at me as if about   90
To skin me scurvily." On Farfarel,
Whose eyes were gleaming with the lust to strike,
Their dean turned sharply and commanded him:
"Away, you filthy bird." The frightened rogue
Resumed then: "Tuscans, Lombards, as you will,   95
I can call hither for you, only let
The band of Badpaws draw aside somewhat
Lest fear of their assault alarm my mates.

155

In me you have but one while on these banks,
Not stirring from this spot, I can call forth   100
Some seven more by whistling, as we do
When one of us has spied the coast is clear."
At this suggestion Dogsnout shook his head
And raised his muzzle, saying: "What a trick
He has devised to duck beneath again!"   105
The crafty scamp, who did not want for wiles,
Made answer: "Cunning you would have me when
I would bring greater suffering on my tribe!"
Here Harlequin tempestuous intervened
Against his comrade, menacing the rogue: 110
"If you dive in again, not on fleet foot
But on swift wing I'll swoop down on the pitch:
We'll leave the rim; you make the bank your screen
And see if you alone can gull us all."

Dispose yourself now, reader, to new sport: 115
Each demon faced the inner crest, he first
Who had been most suspicious of the game;
The Navarrese, his moment choosing well,
Dug in his toes to spring and in a flash
Leaped and was free of their fierce captain's clutch.   120
Crestfallen then stood the frustrated fiends.
Chiefly the demon who had first been duped –
He took off, wings outspread and shouting loud:
"I've got you, rogue!" but vaunted so in vain,
For speed of flight could not outstrip blind fear,   125
And, as the sinner plunged, the wingèd imp
Brushed the black pitch with upward turning breast,
Even as the falcon swoops and skyward veers
Again, betrayed and baffled, when the water fowl
Submerges at the sudden whirr of wings.   130

Demons. *Inferno* XXI–XXII

Irked by the swindle, Frostfoot swiftly flew
Hot after Harlequin, in hope it seemed,
To fight his fellow should the knave escape,
For when the slippery cheat had disappeared
He turned his talons on his brother imp   135
And wrestling they locked above the pond.
His rival was a valiant sparrow-hawk
And gripped him fiercely so the grappling pair
Together plummeted beneath the pitch.
The seething heat dissolved their fierce embrace,   140
But so tar-clotted were their dripping plumes
They could not extricate themselves alone.
In helpless rage the devils' crew stood by,
And Curlybeard bade four to fly with hooks
Across the ditch; straightway on either shore   145
The fiends took up their stand with grappling irons
Extended to the luckless twain entrapped,
Already parboiled 'neath the glue-like crust.

We left them tangled in their self-made toils.

CANTO XXIII

Wordless and solitary we fared on
Without our escort. Virgil trod ahead,
I on his traces, as Franciscans trudge
Along the highway; the mad brawl I'd seen
Had brought the tale of Aesop to my mind   5
Wherein he fables of the rat and frog,
For close comparing showed them similar
From start to finish. And, as may occur
That from one thought another sequent springs,
Reflection brought a fresh conclusion forth   10
That doubled my first fear. I reasoned thus:
On our account the fiends have suffered hurt
And seen themselves the sport of ridicule,
Which mightily must gall them. If now wrath
Be superimposed on their malevolence   15
They will come hotly raging on our scent
Like hounds bare-fanged to rend the hapless hare.
I felt my hair a-bristle with affright
And o'er my shoulder threw an anxious glance,
Calling to Virgil: "Some concealment find   20
For both of us straightway, else must I dread
The Badpaws, launched already in pursuit.
My fancy tells me that I hear them now."
And he to me: "Were I of leaded glass
Your outer image I could not reflect   25
More truly than your inner sense I seize.
Your thought expressed has mingled close with mine,
Alike in act and form; of both our fears
One common counsel have I drawn for us.
If the right bank so slopes as to permit   30
Our access to the next entrenchment, then
We shall escape the fancied chase you fear."

Scarce had he ceased to speak when I beheld
The imps approaching us with outspread wings,
Fast flying and with purpose all too plain.   35
At once my leader seized me, like a mother,
Wakened by sound of flames she sees draw near,
Who snatches up her babe and flees apace
Not so much staying as to don a shift,
Unmindful of herself with mother love.   40
With swifter speed did never water run
Through channelled sluice to turn a land mill's wheel,
Dashing against the paddles than was his
As from the summit of the rocky ridge
Enclosing the sixth hollow on one side   45
He hurled himself and sliding on his back
Descended, bearing me upon his breast,
As were I more than friend, aye, cherished son.
His feet had hardly touched the narrow floor
Of the next pouch when on the ridge the fiends   50
Stood over us – but now we feared them not,
For that high Providence which had ordained
Their sovereignty over the tar-filled foss
Did not permit them to emerge therefrom.

Down here we found a gilded company,   55
Moving along with slow and languid stride,
Dejected, weary and with tearful mien.
Long capes they wore with overhanging hoods
Shading their brows and like in style and cut
To robes in Cluny fashioned for the friars.   60
All overworked in gold of dazzling sheen
They were without, but lined with lead within;
Those Frederick gave 'gainst these would seem as straw.
O weary mantle never to be doffed!

Turning as always to the left, we moved   65
Beside them and their sobbing filled our ears.
So labored was their pace beneath the load
That every step we took brought us abreast
Of new companions, whence I begged my guide:
"As we pass by, try glancing on the file   70
To find some one of these whose name or works
May be familiar to me." Back of us
One heard my Tuscan speech and cried aloud:
"Slacken your pace, I pray you twain who speed
So swiftly through this melancholy air,   75
And what you seek perhaps I may provide."
I stopped and spied a pair whose urgency
To be with us was written on their brows,
But haste was hindered by the narrow path
And weary burden of the weight they bore.   80
When they stood by us first with furtive eye
They scanned me, wordless. Then one, turning, said:
"He seems alive, by throbbing of his throat,
And if not so, then by what privilege
May they walk here without our heavy stole?"   85
Then they addressed me: "Tuscan, who have come
To this harsh college of the hypocrites,
Do not disdain to tell us who you are."
I answered: "Born and bred I was beside
The banks of Arno, noble stream, within   90
The walls of the great city and I wear
The mortal vesture I have worn since birth.
Yourselves disclose, from whose cheeks grief distils
Such bitter flowing tears as I behold,
And whence your iridescent penalty?"   95
And one replied: "Our coruscating cowls
Of orange hue are laden so with lead

163

To set the scales a-creaking with the weight.
Two Gaudent Friars are we, both Bolognese:
I Catalan and Loderingo he.   100
Elected by your city were we twain,
As is the use sometimes to choose but one,
To keep the peace. Such pacifiers were we
As you may see Gardingo witness yet."
"Your sorrows, brothers –," so I made reply   105
But no more uttered, for as I looked down
My eye chanced on a figure crucified
By three stout stakes that nailed him to the ground.
Meeting my glance he strained and writhed about
While broken sobs and panting stirred his beard.   110
Remarking my surprise Fra Catalan
Explained: "The soul impaled you here observe
Is he who counseled to the Pharisees
That one should suffer for the people's sake.
Here lies he, as you see, across the road,   115
Trod on by all, for his doom is to feel
Each sinner's weight as each plods on his round.
In like style in this ditch his kinsman too
Is pilloried with all the counselors
Whose judgment sowed the bitter seed for Jews."   120
He spoke and I saw Virgil in amaze
Gaze down upon the shade spread like a cross
To bear his shame for all eternity.

Then he addressed the Friar: "Tell us, pray,
If it be lawful, does some passage lie   125
On our right hand by which we may depart
Without constraining any dusky fiend
To come and help us issue from this cleft?"
The answer came: "Much nearer than you hope

164

The shade spread like a cross
To bear his shame for all eternity.

Inferno XXIII, 122–123

There stands an outflung rock that from the wall   130
External bridges all these grim ravines,
Save that o'er this its broken span allows
No passage. On its rubble you may climb
Which lies piled up against the inner bank."
Head bowed in thought my leader stood awhile,   135
Then spoke: "A poor account we had from him
Who flays the sinners in the other pouch."
"Long since I learned, in old Bologna's halls,"
Replied the Friar, "that Beelzebub
Has many vices, 'mongst which, I was told,   140
He shuns the truth and fathers every lie."
At this my captain hastily moved on,
His countenance with anger overcast,
And I too left behind the burdened souls
In anxious haste to trace the well loved steps.   145

CANTO XXIV

In the sweet season of the new born year
When the young sun unbinds his locks anew
Beneath the Water-bearer, when the night
Retreating shifts her shadow to the South,
Then, as the hoar frost mocks on field and mead   5
The image of her sister cold and white
(Though short-lived is the temper of her pen),
The needy peasant rises from his rest
And looks abroad to see the countryside
All over whitened, whence he beats his thigh   10
And turns again to seek his cottage walls,
Bemoaning his hard lot, yet soon once more
Emerges and more hopeful harvest gleans,
Seeing the earth change hue in little time;
He rouses then and, seizing his stout crook,   15
Leads out his flock to springtime pasturage.
Such alternation did I undergo;
Alarmed, I saw my master's clouded brow
And felt dismay but soon the poultice came
To soothe the wound, for as we stood beside   20
The broken bridge, he turned to me and smiled
With that same aspect gentle and benign
He bore when we first met beneath the hill.

After some inner counsel, studying well
The fall of rocks, he opened wide his arms   25
And held me in his embrace. Then as one
Who while he acts yet plans the sequent step
So upward raising me toward the top
Of each crag he ascended whilst he eyed
The peak to come and urged me as we climbed: 30
"Take footing there and mount but try it first
If it will bear you." Cumbered with a cape

No man or shade could have climbed upward here,
For we indeed, though he not in the flesh
And I thus aided, scarce won the ascent   35
In laboring stride from stone to steeper stone.
And were it not that on the inner rim
The slope was shorter than the outer bank
My strength had failed – I cannot speak for his.
But since the nature of the place is such   40
That Evilpits toward the lower well
Is sharp inclined, it follows that each pouch
Is walled in higher on the outer edge.
At last we reached the crest of the divide
And from my lungs the breath of life was milked   45
So that no further could I go but once
The summit gained sat helpless to proceed.

"Now," said my master, "indolence dismiss,
For resting upon downy feather-beds
Or under coverlets attains not fame,   50
Without which he who lets his lifetime pass
Leaves such a trace of him upon the earth
As smoke in air or fragile foam at sea.
Arise then and exhaustion overcome
With strength of spirit that wins every war   55
If it be not by sluggish flesh undone.
A steeper stair awaits yet our ascent;
To leave such souls behind is not enough.
If I speak clearly let my word prevail."
I rose up then and strove to show my strength   60
More ready for the road than 'twas in truth,
Saying, "Lead on, for I am fresh and strong."

So we took up our way and toiled again
Along the craggy, rough and narrow path,

Steeper by far than that we'd left behind.   65
I spoke while climbing, hoping to conceal
Fatigue, and from the seventh cleft a voice
Came forth in answer though with words malformed.
I knew not what was said though now I stood
Upon the summit of the bridging arch   70
Yet well could I detect the tone of wrath.
Downward I peered but with my mortal eyes
I could not penetrate the murky depth,
Wherefore I spoke: "Good master, lead our steps
On to the inner bank; let's leave the bridge   75
Whereon I hear but no word understand
And dimly see but nothing may perceive."
"No other answer will I make," said he,
"Save in the act, for a discreet request
Should be so met and not with idle words."   80
So we descended from the bridgehead where
It joined the barrier to the eighth ravine;
Here lay the ditch before me, all too clear.
Herein my eyes beheld a serpents' nest;
So thick in number, so bizarre in form   85
Its reptile denizens that to recall
Their aspect drains my very veins of blood.
Let Libya vaunt no more its dreadful sands,
For though they teem with adders and black asps
And cenchres and two-headed amphisbenes   90
Yet never did their vast extent embrace –
Nay, though thereto be added Ethiop's waste
And all the desert of Arabia –
So vast and varied serpent brood as here
Writhed, hissed and crawled before my frightened eyes.   95
Amidst their venomed menace fear-struck folk,
Naked and helpless, ran and sought in vain

171

For path of flight or saving heliotrope.
Their hands were bound behind their backs by snakes
Twisting in knots and boring through their loins   100
With head and tail to join again in front.

Lo, even as we watched, a serpent sprang
At one who stood close by us and transfixed
His quivering throat where neck and shoulders meet;
And quicker than the pen writes *i* or *o*   105
He blazed in flames and burned and fell consumed,
A heap of crumbling ashes, to the ground,
And from the ashes grew again the shape
To form the man that had stood there before.
(Even in such wise, as ancient scholars tell,   110
The Phoenix burns and grows to birth again
When full five hundred years he has fulfilled;
Throughout his life no grain nor grass he eats
But feeds on balsam and on incense tears,
And nard and myrrh he makes his winding sheet.)   115
And as a man who felled by force unknown,
Either by fiend within who strikes him down
Or in convulsive fit that racks his frame,
When he stands up again will gaze about
Bemused and shattered by the recent shock   120
And gazing slowly sigh, so here the wretch,
Thus ruined and restored, stood stupefied.
Almighty Power of God, what strength is Thine
To deal on errant souls such vengeful blows!

My leader asked the sinner whence he came.   125
"But shortly since," he said, "from Tuscany
I plummeted into this savage gulch.
The bestial not the human life I loved,

172

Their hands were bound behind their backs by snakes
Twisting in knots and boring through their loins.

Inferno XXIV, 99–100

Mule that I was. I'm Vanni Fucci, brute;
Pistoia was for me a fitting lair."   130
I cried out then: "See he slip not away,
And ask him what misdeed has brought him here
For I knew him as violent and cruel."
The sinner, hearing me, shrank not aside
But turned his face attentive toward my own   135
While shade of sorry guilt bedecked his cheek.
He snarled: "More grief I feel that thus entrapped
You find me in my shame than that I felt
When I was ravished from the life above.
Yet may I not refuse what you request: 140
Thus deeply down I dwell because I stole
The precious trappings from the sacristy
Though falsely was the guilt elsewhere assigned.
But, so you may not glory in this sight,
If ever you come forth from our dim land,   145
Open your ears and hear my prophecy.
Pistoia first grows lean of Blacks, whereat
Your Florence changes families and laws;
From Val di Magra Mars calls forth a bolt
Enveloped in thick clouds. The tempest breaks   150
Wild and impetuous while clash of arms
Re-echoes from Piceno. Then the bolt
With sudden fury will disperse the clouds
And every White will suffer injury.
This I reveal that it may bring you pain."   155

CANTO XXV

When he had said his say the thieving soul
Raised both hands high and made the figging sign,
Shouting aloud: "Take this, God; this for you!"
Thenceforward I looked on the snakes as friends
For straightway one wound tight around his neck   5
As if to say, "No more; that's quite enough."
Another ringed his arms and bound them fast
In tangled convolutions so the thief
Could scarcely move his shoulders in a shrug.
Ah, impious Pistoia, should you not   10
Decree to raze yourself with purging flame
Since in ill-doing you surpass your seed?
In all the darkling circles of deep Hell
I found no soul so insolent toward God –
Not even him struck down from high-walled Thebes.   15

He fled and uttered forth no further sound
And I beheld a centaur raging come,
Crying, "Where is he now, the foul-mouthed lout?"
Not in Maremma, I believe, are found
Such countless serpents as his body bore;   20
Save for his face they covered him entire.
Above his shoulders, straight upon the nape
There crouched a dragon with outspreading wings
Whose hot breath sets to blazing where it breathes.
My master said: "'Tis Cacus we see here,   25
Who often neath the caves of Aventine,
Rending his helpless prey, make lakes of blood.
He hunts not with his fellows up above
For thief he was and made the treacherous theft
Of the great flock that pastured near his cave   30
And so brought to an end his evil work
Under the club of Hercules who dealt

Him five score blows though he felt less than ten."
While thus he spoke and the blasphemer fled
Three spirits had approached and stood near us,   35
Nor had we noted them save when they spoke
And challenged, "Who are you?" Our colloquy
We interrupted to lend ear to them.
I knew them not but it so came about,
As often happens in a dialogue,   40
That one had need to use another's name,
Inquiring, "Cianfa, where can he have gone?"
On this, to caution silence to my chief
I laid a warning finger on my lips.
If you are loath now, Reader, to believe   45
What I shall tell I will not be surprised
For I who saw it scarce can credit sight.
Even as I bent my brow to look on them
A fearful six-legg'd snake came forth and hurled
Himself upon one thief and held him fast   50
From top to toe; his paunch the middle limbs
Close grappled and his arms the upper paws,
Biting the wretch meanwhile on both his cheeks.
The reptile's nether limbs wound round his thighs
While twixt the sinner's legs the tail was thrust   55
To curl up sharp behind the trembling loins.
Never was ivy so entwined to tree
As were the serpent's limbs upon the man.
Then did they fuse as they had been of wax
And mixed the serpentine and human hues   60
And neither was what it had been before,
Just as a moving barrier of brown
Not yet charred black and yet no longer white
Precedes the fire on a burning page,
The other two looked on and cried in fright: 65

Biting the wretch meanwhile on both his cheeks.
The reptile's nether limbs wound round his thighs
While twixt the sinner's legs the tail was thrust
To curl up sharp behind the trembling loins.

Inferno xxv, 53–56

"Agnel, alas what fearful change is this?
You are not two and yet no longer one."
The two heads merged and in one face confused
The features of the monster and the man
Were intermingled while two uncouth limbs   70
From coalescence of the human arms
With reptile forelegs the new Thing acquired;
Its thighs and nether limbs and paunch became
Such monstrous forms as never eye had seen.
All former features blurred of snake and man,   75
And seeming neither and yet weirdly both,
The creature staggered off with heavy stride.

And as the lizard, under the great scourge
Of summer's heat, darting from hedge to hedge
Moves like a lightning flash across the road,   80
So here a little serpent burning bright,
All black and livid like a peppercorn,
Leaped toward the bellies of the other two,
Transfixing one just in that vital spot
Whence yet unborn we draw our nourishment,   85
Then fell down spent, distended at his feet.
The stricken shade said nought but fixed his eye
Upon the serpent, then he gave a yawn
As if assailed by fever or fatigue.
Now snake eyed man and man returned the gaze   90
While smoke curled upward from the reptile's mouth
And from the wounded belly of the thief
And the two vapors merged. Let Lucan vaunt
In vain Sabellus and Nisidius,
Nay rather let him listen in amaze;   95
Let Ovid speak no word of Cadmus here
Nor Arethusa; though he changes man

To serpent form and maiden to a fount
I yield not to him. Ne'er did he transmute
Two different natures standing face to face   100
Nor ever see two unlike forms exchanged,
Each substance quick to take the other's stamp.
Together step by step they were transformed:
The serpent's tail was split fork-shaped for legs,
The hapless felon's feet were then conjoined,   105
With legs and thighs in one mass fused compact.
The tail divided took on human shapes
Even as they vanished from the stricken knave;
The snake's skin softened and the man's grew scales.
Retracted through the pits the sinner's arms   110
Quite disappeared, the while the snake's forepaws
Stretched out in measure as the other's shrank.
His hindmost legs were twisted in one skein
To make the man-like member shame conceals;
His own the sorry wretch saw split in twain   115
To form two feet. Beneath the smoke each changed
His tint to his new state; the vapor brought
Hair forth on one and stripped it from the other.
Then did one mingled creature, man no more,
Fall to the earth, the other stood erect   120
Yet neither shifted gaze from other's eyes,
While heads transposed to match each new-made shape.
He who stood upright drew his snakes snout in,
Back toward the temples and the ears sprang out,
Of excess substance drawn from hollowed cheeks   125
While of the stuff remaining came the nose
And lips puffed out to seemly measurement.
The other, lying prone, pushed forth his snout,
Withdrawing his once human ears within
The skull as timid snails retract their horns.   130

180

His tongue at first all one and apt for speech
Was cloven in two parts; the upright thing
Felt his forked tongue made whole – and the smoke cleared.
The adder-soul that recently was man
Went hissing through the valley; hard behind   135
The new man chased him, spitting as he went.
Then he stopped short to turn his new formed back
And tell his mate remaining, "As I ran
Writhing on this rock floor let Buoso run."

Such shifting transmutations I observed   140
Among the ballast of the seventh hold.
If here my pen run wild, let novelty
Of such weird sights my exculpation be.
Although my eyes were mazed and wit confused
Yet could the wretches not so fast escape   145
That I could fail to know them. Puccio he
Who suffered no reptilian change of all
The trio, while the third was that base knave
Who still, Gaville, gives you cause for tears.

CANTO XXVI

Rejoice, my Florence, in your glorious fame:
On land and sea your banners wave unfurled
And down in darkest Hell your name is known.
Amongst the thieves three Florentines I found
Such as to make me blush for shame, and you   5
Reap no great honor from these citizens.
But if true dreams come just before the dawn
Then shortly will you feel the avenging blows
That Prato – aye and others – crave for you.
Had vengeance struck ere now 'twere not too soon.   10
Since it must be I would 'twere done; each year
That passes makes it bitterer to bear.
We went our way; the jagged cliff made stairs
On which my chief ascended, leading me;
And feet alone served not, but with hands too   15
We labored up the bleak and rugged slope.
The grief that seized me then I feel anew
When I recall the sight that met my eyes;
Remembering, I keep tighter rein on wit
Than is my wont, lest it may run unchecked   20
By virtue's guidance, so that if perchance
Some favoring star or nobler arbiter
Has blessed me with a talent, I myself
May not misuse it to my own dismay.

As on the hill the idle peasant lies   25
In summer time, when he who lights the world
Less of his visage masks to mortal eyes,
Resting from labor as the night comes on
(While flies give way to buzzing hordes of gnats),
And sees the valley where he toils and ploughs   30
Sparkling with myriad moving lights, so here
The eighth entrenchment glowed with flickering flares

185

Apparent when I stood above its gulf.
And as the prophet whom the bears avenged
Beheld Elijah lifted heavenward,   35
Watching as steeds his chariot bore aloft
In such a swift and glorious upward flight
That only rising radiance he beheld
In cloud-cloaked splendor mounting to the sky,
In such guise did each errant flame move on   40
Along the bottom of the shadowed gorge
And none reveals the burden borne within,
But every flame enshrouds a sinner's soul.
I stood upright upon the bridge above,
Leaning to look; had I not seized a crag   45
I might have fallen though no hand had pushed.
My teacher who beheld me so absorbed
Explained: "Within the fire the spirits dwell,
Each one close swathed in burning robes of flame."
"By your assurance, master," I replied,   50
"I am made certain, but my concept was
Already clear and fain was I to ask
Who moves within the fire forked above
And seeming like the flame that rose two-tongued
From out the funeral pyre which consumed   55
The Theban brothers, each by other slain."
He answered: "In that flame are Diomed
And sly Ulysses punished, suffering both
Together Heaven's vengeance, as of old
Together they went forth on their forays.   60
Repentance is exacted for the horse
By stratagem of which the gate was made
Whence issued forth the noble seed of Rome,
And tears of vain regret are yet distilled
For cruel betrayal of Achilles' spouse,   65

186

In that flame are Diomed
And sly Ulysses punished.

Inferno XXVI, 57–58

Who even in death still mourns their guileful trick,
And for the raped Palladium here they pay."
"If here, though flame-encircled, they may speak,
Then, master," so I urged, "I do implore
And will a thousand times beseech your aid   70
That you may not my pleading hear in vain,
But let the two-horned flame draw near to us;
See now with what desire I lean toward it."

He made reply: "Right worthy is your plea
Of every praise and I shall grant it you.   75
But say no more and leave all words to me,
For I have well in mind what you would hear
While they, who once were Greeks, would shy away
Perhaps from your speech."
                              When the flame stood close
My guide seized the occasion as it came   80
And while I listened he addressed them thus:
"O burning twain within one fire consumed,
If I earned well of you while yet I lived,
If much or little you esteemed my pen
When in the living world my lofty lines   85
I wrote of you, now stay and pass not by
But let one tell of his last journey's end."

The higher horn of that most ancient flame
Now fell to undulation, crepitant,
As fire will when whipped up by the wind.   90
Thence, as the blazing point moved back and forth,
Even as a tongue that shapes the spoken word,
The hero's voice emerged to tell his tale:
"When I took leave of Circe who had kept me
By her side yonder near Gaeta's shore   95

187

(Before Aeneas had so named the place),
No thought of my sweet son nor reverence
For my old father nor the love that should
Long since have comforted Penelope
Could overcome the zeal that burned in me   100
To seek an expert's knowledge of the world
And of the vice and valor of mankind.
Nay, I set forth on the deep open sea,
With one ship only and that little band
Of comrades who had not forsaken me.   105
As far as Spain, far as Morocco's coast
I saw both shores, saw too Sardinia
And the other isles laved by our inland sea.
I and my shipmates were both old and tired
When we came finally to that narrow strait   110
Where Hercules had set his frontier posts
So that no man should ever go beyond:
I left Seville behind me on my right,
As on the other side I'd left Ceuta.
'Brothers,' I said, 'who through a hundred thousand   115
Dangers have reached at last the setting sun,
To this, the last brief vigil of your senses
That yet remains to you, do not deny
Experience of that unpeopled world
Which lies beyond the sun, unknown to all.   120
Reflect upon the seed from which you spring:
You were not made to live the lives of brutes,
But rather to seek virtue and to learn.'
With this brief exhortation I aroused
My comrades to such keenness for the voyage   125
That I could not have stopped them if I would.
So, turning toward the morning sky our stern,
We made wings of our oars for the mad flight,

Keeping the while our course turned toward the left.
Now night disclosed to us the other pole   130
With all its stars attendant, while our own
Lay low submerged beneath the ocean floor.
Five times the splendor underneath the moon
Had been relighted and as often dimmed
Since we had started on our lofty course,   135
When there appeared to us a mountain, dark
Because far distant, yet, I thought, so high
That I had never seen its like. We then
Rejoiced but joy turned speedily to grief
For from that new-found land a whirlwind came   140
And struck upon the forepart of our bark;
Three times with all the waves it spun her round
With the fourth turn it lifted up her poop
And downward forced her bow (as it pleased One)
Until the sea closed over ship and all."   145

CANTO XXVII

The flickering tongue was still and stood upright,
Forming no further word, and moved away,
Granted dismissal by my courteous bard.
When lo, another, pressing close behind,
Drew our eyes to its summit whence came forth   5
A crepitation muted and confused.
As once the iron bull of Sicily,
Whose first sad lowing issued from the throat
Of him who had first cast the brazen beast
(As was but right), was wont to shape its roars   10
From lamentations of the wretch inside,
So that although the monster was of bronze
Yet did he seem to suffer fleshly pain,
So here the heavy syllables of grief,
Having no issue from the sinner's mouth,   15
Were altered into crackling of fire.
But once the uttered words had reached the tip
The flame was whipped to shape them as a tongue
And we heard clearly:
                          "You I charge, O soul
Who spoke just now in Lombard when you said,   20
'Be on your way, no more I seek of you.'
Though tardily I come to beg my boon
Let it not burden you to stay and speak;
See that it irks not me although I burn.
If into this dark world you have but now   25
Come down from that sweet Latin land above
Whence I brought all my guilt, then tell, I pray,
If peace or war the Romagnoli have.
I come from where the mountains rise to cut
Urbino from the slopes whence Tiber springs."   30
I still stood bent attentive and spoke not,
But Virgil nudged me, whispering in my ear:

193

"A Latin 'tis who asks; do you reply."
And I, having my answer all prepared,
Straightway began to speak without delay: 35
"O soul, down in concealment there, your land,
Romagna, is not now nor ever was
Free of the wars that fill its tyrants' hearts,
But when I left no war raged openly.
Ravenna stands as she has stood for years,   40
The eagle of Polenta broods there still,
Still shading Cervia with its wings. The city
That once endured the long ordeal and made
A bloodstained heap of the defeated French
Now finds itself again 'neath the green claws.   45
The mastiffs of Verrucchio, young and old,
Who with Montagna dealt so wickedly,
Where is their wont still make their teeth an auger.
The towns of the Lamone and Santerno
Follow the lion cub of the white lair,   50
Who with the changing seasons changes sides.
The one whose flank is bathed by Savio's waters
Even as she lies between the plain and mountain
So lives between free state and tyranny.
Now who you are I ask you to disclose;   55
Be not obdurate more than others are,
So may your name on earth bear its head high."
The flame then hissed and purred as was its wont
And moved its glowing point from side to side
Forming the words that follow:
                              "If I thought   60
My answer made to one who ever might
Return again up to the living world
This fiery tongue would motionless remain.
But since no living soul has ever left

194

BONIFACE·
·VIII·

The prince of the new sect of Pharisees.

Inferno XXVII, 84

This pit of Hell, if I hear true report,   65
I dare to answer without fear of shame.
Soldier I was, then put on Francis' cord,
Thinking, thus girt, for my sins to atone,
And surely would my hope have been fulfilled
Had not the High Priest, whom the Devil take,   70
Set me again on ways of early fault,
And how and why this was I shall disclose.
While yet I wore the bones and mortal flesh
My mother gave me, all my earthly deeds
Partook not of the lion but the fox.   75
Sharp stratagem and wily subterfuge,
I knew them well and practised so their use
That my repute was spread abroad the world.
At length, when I had reached that stage of life
When men should furl their sail and clew their sheets,   80
Then what I once enjoyed gave me regret
And shriven penitent I penance made
And stood to save myself – but hear the rest.
The prince of the new sect of Pharisees
Meanwhile was waging war near Lateran –   85
And not with pagan Saracen nor Jew,
For every foeman was of Christian faith
And none had had a hand in Acre's fall
Nor trafficked with the Sultan's infidels.
Respecting not his own high eminence   90
Nor Holy Orders and accounting nought
The bridle that once made its wearers lean,
But as within Soracte Constantine
To heal his taint sought Saint Sylvester out,
So he called me as doctor in his need   95
To cure him of his feverish arrogance.
Counsel he asked of me; but I was still,

For like a drunkard's ravings seemed his speech.
But yet he pressed me, urging 'Let your heart
Be not afraid, for absolution now   100
I give you, only show me how I may
Raze stubborn Palestrina to the ground.
The gates of Heaven, as you know full well,
I open wide or close, as I desire,
For my hand holds the double keys whose worth   105
My predecessor chose not to esteem.'
His urgent arguments so shook my will
That silence seemed the worser choice. I spoke:
'Since, Father, you absolve me of that sin
In which I am to fall, this counsel take: 110
A generous promise with fulfilment scant
Will bring you triumph on your lofty throne.'
Saint Francis came for me as I lay dead
But a black cherub checked him, crying out:
'Nay, take him not away, you do me wrong;   115
He must come down and join my retinue
Because of counsel fraudulent he gave.
E'er since that day I've waited by his side.
He who repents not may not be absolved
Nor can repentance coexist with will   120
To sin: The law of contradictories
Will not allow it.' Ah, my hapless lot!
How fearfully I shuddered as I felt
The fiend's hand hard on me and heard his voice:
'You little thought, perhaps, to find in me   125
A good logician.' Then he bore me off
To Minos and that hideous judge eight times
Wrapped his long tail about himself and, lashed
To frenzy, bit himself in wrath and cried:
'This culprit merits well the burning shroud.'   130

196

Hence, damned to suffer as you see me now,
And still resentful, I go clothed in fire."

When he had finished his sad history
The flame, still moaning, went upon its way,
The sharp point ever darting restlessly.   135

We moved on then, I and my noble guide,
Along the rocky bank, and soon bestrode
The other arch that crosses the deep gulch
Where discord sowers pay their frightful fee
And where schismatics answer for their guilt.   140

CANTO XXVIII

What chronicler could hope to give account
Of all the blood and wounds that I saw here?
Nay, though the tale were told and told again
In syllables uncramped by rules of verse
Yet still no human tongue could set it forth: 5
Sheer weight of horror upon horror piled
Would overtax our speech while mortal mind
Lacks scope to grasp their terrible extent.
If every mangled corpse that bled of old
On the Apulian plain ploughed by the wars   10
Of Trojan waging and the later strife
So long enduring when a mighty crop
Of Roman rings was reaped (as Livy tells,
Who may not err), and if thereto were joined
The mutilated host of those who fell   15
Vainly resisting Robert Guiscard's sword
(Whose bones the passerby yet comes upon
At Ceperano where Apulia's knights
Were faithless and on Tagliacozzo's field
Which sly Alardo won by stratagem) –   20
If all the myriads mangled in those frays
Were brought together and each showed his stump
Or bleeding gash, still were the spectacle
Surpassed by the grim aspect of this vale.

A cask, reft of its midboard or its cant,   25
Leaks not more badly than one soul I saw
Ripped open clear from anus up to chin.
Pendant his guts swung down between his legs,
The pluck appeared and that unlovely sack
Which turns our nourishment to excrement,   30
And, as I fixed my fascinated gaze
Upon him, he looked up and with his hands
Wide opened his reft breast and spoke to me:

"Behold how I am rent, see how undone
Mahomet is. Before me Ali treads,   35
Head split asunder from the brow to chin.
We and the others that you look upon
Were seeds of schism in the life above
And scandal sowers, hence are we so clipped.
A fiend stands farther back who dresses us   40
In such a fashion as you here behold,
And as we circle all our wounds are healed
So when the pain-racked round is done, again
He wields his ax and gashes us afresh.
But who are you thus lingering on the bridge,   45
Reluctant it may be to meet the pain
Assigned to you in judgment for your fault?"
"Not yet death's prisoner," my chief replied,
"Nor hither brought to suffer smart for sin,
He comes to seek full knowledge of your world.   50
I, who no longer live, fulfill my charge
To shepherd him from ring to ring of Hell;
I tell the truth as sure as I stand here."
More than a hundred when they heard him speak
Stopped in their tracks amazed to look on me,   55
Forgetting, for a while, their suffering.
"Since then it may be you will see the sun
Ere long, tell Fra Dolcino to provide
His flock with victuals, lest beset by snows
He yield the victory to the Novarese   60
And join me here below. If he but heed
He may not easily be overcome."
Even as he spoke Mahomet held up-raised
One foot and as he ended brought it down
And took his leave.
     Another with pierced throat,   65

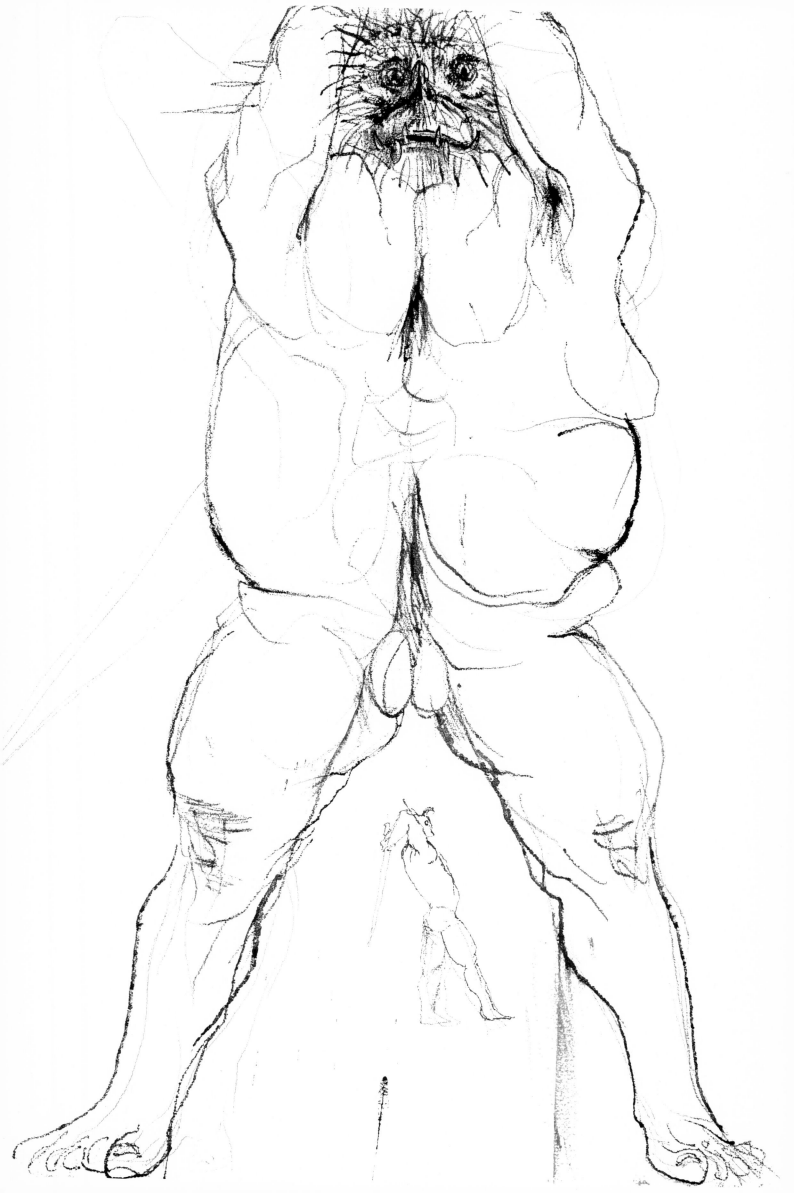

A fiend stands further back who dresses us
In such a fashion.

Inferno XXVIII, 40–41

Nose lopped off to the brow and one ear gone
Stayed with the rest to marvel as he gaped
And opened up his windpipe which, laid bare,
Showed crimson stained on either side, and said:
"O soul, through no transgression hither sent 70
And whom, if chance resemblance tricks me not,
I knew sometime on earth in Latin lands,
Remember Pier da Medicina when
You view once more the gently rolling plain
That from Vercelli slopes to Marcabò. 75
And warn the two best men of Fano town,
Ser Guido and good Angiolello both,
That if infernal foresight be not vain
They are to be cast over their ship's side
Off Point Cattólica and foully drowned 80
Through a fell tyrant's treacherous design.
Never twixt Cyprus and Majorca's shore
Did ever Neptune witness such offence
Not by piratical nor Argive hands.
That traitor who has but one eye to see 85
And whose domains my comrade standing here
Could wish his sight ne'er rested on will call
To parley the all-unsuspecting pair
And then will so dispose that prayer nor vow
They need not offer 'gainst Focara's gales." 90
"Explain and show to me," I answered him,
"If you would have me speak of you on earth,
Who is your fellow of regretful sight."
Then putting forth his hand he clutched the jaw
Of one beside him, prying wide his mouth 95
And cried: "This is the man, though he speaks not.
'Twas he who, exiled, banished Caesar's doubt,
Affirming that the party best prepared

Never to its advantage waits on time."
How woebegone and sad did Curio seem,   100
With tongue cut out from his mouth's cavity,
He once so bold and daring in his speech!

Next one appeared with both hands chopped away
And raising his two stumps in that dark air
So high the blood befouled his face, he cried: 105
"You will remember Mosca too on earth;
I, luckless wretch, pronounced the fateful phrase
'A thing done has an end' that was the seed
Of evil fruit for all the Tuscan folk."
"And death to your own kin," I added, whence   110
Accumulating woe on woe he went
As one grief-maddened on his weary round.

I lingered yet a while to eye the crowd
And saw a thing I should be loath to tell
On my own warrant without further proof   115
Save that my conscience gives me confidence,
Conscience, that comrade that uplifts our hearts
When armored by its conscious purity.
For I did see and seem to see again
A headless trunk move slowly on its way   120
In like pace as the others of that herd.
Clutching the hair, a hand bore on the head
Which like a lantern swung beside the trunk.
It looked on us and "Woe is me!" it sighed.
So the dismembered being led itself   125
And Two-in-one it was or One-in-two;
How this may be He knows, Who made it so.
I watched it. When it stood beneath the bridge
It raised the arm and held the head aloft

Clutching the hair, a hand bore on the head
Which like a lantern swung beside the trunk.

Inferno XXVIII, 122–123

To bring the nearer to us its lament: 130
"Still breathing soul who walk amidst the dead,
Look on this fashion of dire punishment
And see if there be others like to mine.
So that you may take back report of me
Learn that I am Bertran de Born who gave 135
The evil counsel to the youthful king;
Son against sire I set in such discord
As with his wicked goads Ahithophel
'Twixt Absolom and David did arouse.
Because between two kinsmen joined by blood 140
I made division, here my brain I bear
Divided from its root in this my trunk;
So mark in me the law of like for like."

CANTO XXIX

The sight of wounds so numerous and diverse
Intoxicated my bewildered eyes;
I would have stayed to weep but Virgil said:
"Why does your vision linger so absorbed
Upon the sorry swarm of mangled shades?   5
'Twas not your custom in the other rings.
Consider, if you hope to count them all,
That here the valley measures in its sweep
Full two and twenty miles; meanwhile the moon
Is now beneath us: little time is left   10
And other sights remain for you to see."
"Had you but given heed to why I gazed
Perhaps you had condoned a longer stay,"
So did I answer as we moved again
Upon our journey, Virgil in the lead,   15
And added: "Deep in darkness of that trench
Which was the object of my scrutiny
A spirit of my own blood-kin I think
Bewails the fault so cruelly punished there."
Replied my master: "Let your mind no more   20
Be fixed on him; attend to other things
And leave him where he stands. Beneath the bridge
I saw him threaten you with upraised fist
And heard his fellows speak of him by name,
Geri del Bello, while you gazed enthralled   25
Upon the chatelain of Hautefort,
And as you saw him not he went his way."
"O master mine, the violent death he died,"
I answered, "that as yet is unavenged
By any clansman sharing in the shame   30
Made him resentful; therefore did he go
No word exchanging with me, as I think,
And so compassion stirring in my heart."

209

Conversing in this wise we came at length
To that point on the bridge whence might be viewed   35
If not for lack of light the next ravine
Clear to the bottom. Presently we stood
High o'er the final close of Evilpits
And easily surveyed its brotherhood,
My ears with lamentations were assailed,   40
Sharp darts with cutting edge of pity tipped,
So that I cupped my ears to shut them out.

If all the ills that fill the lazarets
Of Valdichiana when the summer strikes
Together with the legion of the sick   45
Spawned by Maremma and Sardinia
Were in one ditch assembled, such a throng
Might equal, not exceed, the stricken mass
I saw before me. From them came a stench
As if thrown off by rotting flesh and limbs.   50
We made our way down to the lower bank
Of the great crag and turning toward the left
My vision of the pocket grew more keen.
Here in its deep recess the minister
Of God Almighty, Justice Absolute,   55
Deals chastisement to those who in this life
He marks as falsifiers. No sadder sight
Aegina offered when its denizens
Were plague-struck one and all and the foul air
Blighted all life down to the meanest worm,   60
(Then ancient mankind, as the poets tell
Restored itself through seed of ants) than here
It was to see the souls in the dark vale
Piled each on each in helpless, aching heaps.
Some lay extended prone, some on their backs,   65

210

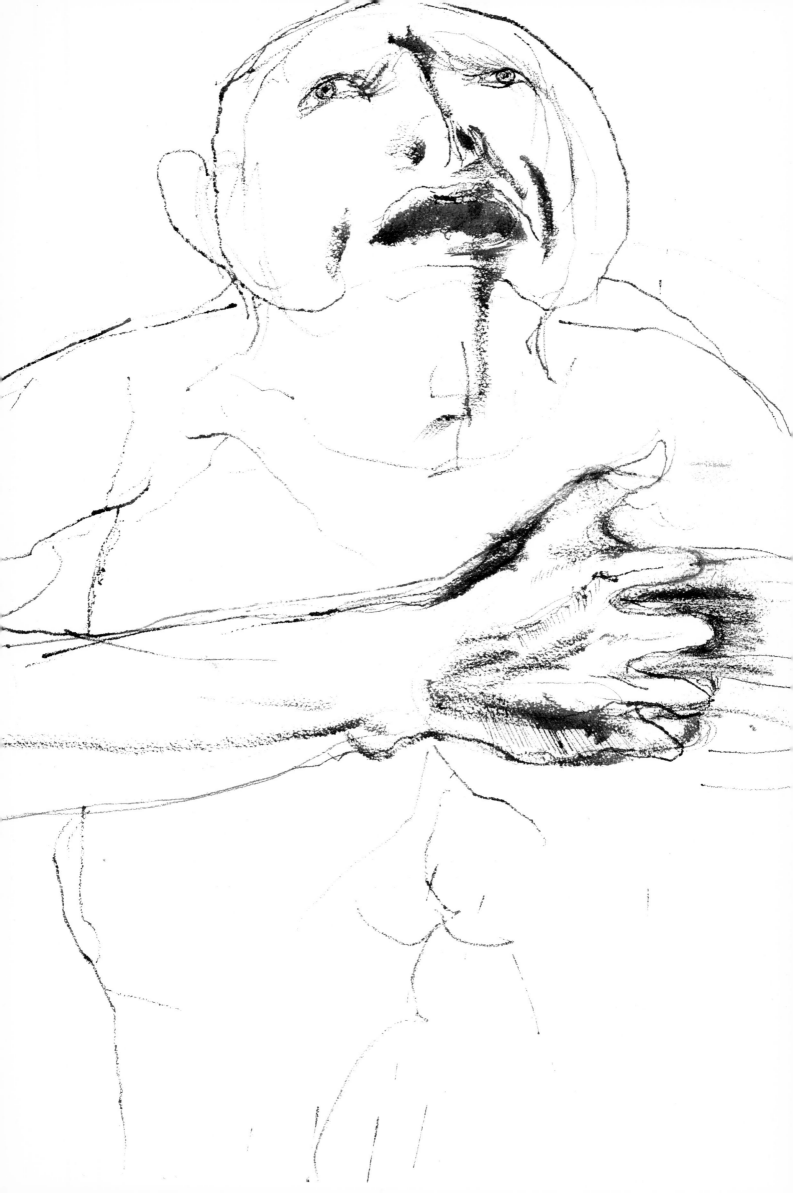

Plied thick upon themselves their furious nails
Seeking relief from their tormenting itch.

Inferno XXIX, 77–78

Prostrated, others rested on their mates,
Some dragged their fevered frames from spot to spot.

Slowly we walked along and silently
We looked and listened to the helpless sick
Who lacked the strength to raise their ailing bones.   70
Two met my eye, one 'gainst the other propped
As saucepans leaning each on each to dry,
Both marked with scabby sores from top to toe,
And ne'er did ostler ply his currycomb
Under his master's eye or 'gainst his will   75
Kept from his bed, with speedier stroke than these
Plied thick upon themselves their furious nails
Seeking relief from their tormenting itch.
And as they scratched the scabby skin flaked off
As scales beneath the knife fall from the bream   80
Or any other fish of large-scaled skin.
"O you, who with your fingers go unscaling
Yourself," my master said to one of them,
"And sometimes plying them in style of pincers,
Tell us if there be any Latin soul   85
Among you here, so may you hope your nails
May for this labor serve eternally."
"Latins are we, whom you behold so wasted –
Aye, both of us," one answered as he wept.
"But who are you, to ask about our state?"   90
My leader said: "I am one who descends
Down with this living man from ledge to ledge,
Purposing to exhibit Hell to him."
Then was undone their mutual support
And, trembling, both turned to me – with others   95
On whose ears the reply had ricocheted.
Then my good master, drawing close to me,

211

Said: "Speak out now and tell them what you want."
And I began, since he had given permission:
"So may your memory not fade away,   100
In the first world, out of the minds of men
But rather long live on through many suns,
Pray tell us who you are and of what clan.
Let not your ugly and unseemly pain
Make you afraid to speak freely to me."   105
"Arezzo was my home, and Albero da Siena,"
One of them answered, "caused me to be burned;
But what I died for did not bring me here.
The truth is, I once told him – all in jest –
That I could rise up in the air in flight.   110
He, having eagerness and little sense,
Because I failed to make him Daedalus
Had his dear father put me to the stake.
But it was for my use of alchemy
That to the last of the ten evil pits   115
Minos condemned me – he who cannot err."
I said then to the poet: "Was there ever
A folk as silly as the Sienese?
Nay, even Frenchmen are less so by far."
Whereat the other leper, hearing me,   120
Answered my observation, "Save for Stricca,
Who learned to moderate expenditures
And Niccolò, the first man to invent
The costly use of cloves – and in that garden
Where such good seed most readily takes root.   125
And save the band in which Caccia d'Ascián
Squandered away the vineyards and the woods
And in which Abbagliato showed his wit.
But so you'll know who it is that seconds you
Against the Sienese, look sharp at me   130

212

So that my face may give you clear reply
And you will see I am Capocchio's shade;
I made false metals with my alchemy
And if I eye you right, you should remember
How excellently I played nature's ape." 135

CANTO XXX

One reached Capocchio and in his neck
Fixed fangs so deeply.

Inferno xxx, 25–26

When Juno was enraged 'gainst Theban blood
Because of Semele, as more than once
She showed, then Athamas became so crazed
That as he saw his wife, on either arm
Bearing a son, approach he roared: "Spread wide   5
The net so I may catch the lioness
With both cubs at the pass," and, stretching out
His arms with talons pitiless, he seized
The one child named Learchus, whirled him 'round
And dashed him 'gainst a rock, whereat his spouse   10
The other with herself drowned in the sea.
And when Fate struck proud Troy, once so assured,
With one blow humbling both king and realm,
Then Hecuba, sad, captive and forlorn,
Fresh from the sight of slain Polyxena,   15
When she espied her Polydorus dead
Upon the shore, for very madness bayed
Like any dog, so sorrow wrung her soul.
But never Furies or of Troy or Thebes
Were guilty of an act so inhumane   20
Even in goading brutes much less men's limbs
As I beheld performed by two pale shades
All naked who ran biting right and left
Like to the boar when thrust out from his sty.
One reached Capocchio and in his neck   25
Fixed fangs so deeply that it dragged him on
Scraping his belly on the hard earth floor.
The Aretine all trembling left alone
To me disclosed: "That rabid little gnome
Is Gianni Schicchi, who in maddened rage   30
Goes goring other souls." And I to him:
"So may his partner's teeth leave you untouched
Say who it is before it skip away."

217

The answer came: "Yon is the ancient shade
Of vicious Myrrha who beyond the bounds   35
Of rightful love felt passion for her sire.
With sinful purpose she would visit him
Taking another's likeness as did he
Who now departs, intending so to win
The lady of the troop. He falsified   40
Buoso Donati, drawing up his will
And validating his last testament."

My eye, which I had fixed on them, I turned
To look upon the other ill-born knaves.
And one I saw whose shape was like a lute,   45
Or would have been if but his groin were lopped
Just where the human trunk is bifurcate.
Grave dropsy with its humors ill-absorbed
Distorting so the members that the face
Bears not its right proportion to the paunch   50
Forced him to hold his opened lips apart
As does the fevered sufferer who curls
For thirst one lip toward chin, the other up.
"O souls who find yourselves in this grey world
Yet free of punishment – I know not why –"   55
Said he to us, "look here, and mark you well
The misery of Master Adam's shade.
Alive all that I wished I had, and now
One little drop of water do I crave.
The winding brooks that from the fresh green hills   60
Of Casentino down to Arno run,
So sweetly trickling on their cooling course,
Are still before my eyes and not in vain,
For their remembered image parches me
More than this ill that wastes my face of flesh.   65

218

The rigid justice searching out my guilt
Draws its occasion from the scene of sin
To stimulate my sighs to quicker flight.
For there Romena stands where the alloy
That bears the Baptist's seal I falsified,   70
Wherefore I left my body burnt above.
But if I could find here the caitiff soul
Of Guido, Alexander, or their brother
I would not trade that sight for Branda's spring.
Already one is with us if those shades   75
That run about in madness speak the truth;
But with bound limbs what profits that to me?
If I were but less swollen by so much
That I could move an inch a century
I would ere now have started in pursuit   80
To seek them out midst this misshapen folk –
Yea, though the circle sweeps eleven miles
And spans not less than half a mile across.
Because of them I'm counted in this crew,
For they it was who led me to engrave   85
The florins with three carats of alloy."
And I to him: "Who are those two poor wretches
Steaming like soaking hands in wintertime,
Huddled together on your right frontier?"
"I found them here – and they have not budged since –   90
When I came hurtling down to this ravine,
Nor do I think they'll move forevermore.
One is the soul who, lying, accused Joseph,
The other is Sinon, the false Greek from Troy:
Their burning fever makes them cast such stench."   95
And one of them who perhaps took it ill
To hear himself alluded to so darkly
With clenched fist punched him in his ugly paunch

Which rumbled like a beaten drum. Whereat
In his turn Master Adam clipped his face   100
With an arm stroke, as hard as he'd received,
And said to him: "Though I may be deprived
Of movement by the grossness of my limbs,
Yet I've an arm free for such jobs as this."
The other answering said: "Not half so prompt   105
You had it when they dragged you to the fire
But so and more you had it when you coined."
The dropsy case retorted: "You speak truth,
But you were hardly such a trusty witness
When you were questioned for the truth at Troy."   110
"If I spoke false you falsified the coinage,"
Sinon replied, "and I'm here for one sin
And you for more than any other fiend."
"Remember, perjurer, the wooden horse,"
Replied the sinner of the swollen belly,   115
"And let it gall you that the whole world knows it."
"And gall you may that thirst," the Greek rejoined,
"Which cracks your tongue, and all the rotten water
That makes your paunch a hedge before your eyes."
The coiner then struck back: "As usual   120
Your mouth cracks open to your own dismay,
For if I'm thirsty and this humor bloats me
You have the fever and an aching head,
And for a chance to lick Narcissus' glass
You'd need but scanty words of invitation."   125

I, listening to them, stood fascinated
When my good master said to me: "See here,
I am not far from falling out with you!"
Hearing him in wrath address himself to me
I turned me to him, full of such deep shame   130

And one I saw whose shape was like a lute.

Inferno xxx, 45

As even now stirs in my memory.
And as is one who dreams of his own hurt
And dreaming wishes it were but a dream,
Desiring what is as if it were not,
So I became, incapable of speech   135
And yearning to excuse myself, the while
I did so and could not believe I did.
"Less shame has washed away a greater fault,"
My master said, "than yours has been; therefore
Cast off the idle burden of regret.   140
But think of me as ever at your side
If henceforth it may hap that fortune place you
Where there are folk in such dispute as this,
For liking to hear such things is a low taste."

CANTO XXXI

The selfsame tongue that first had wounded me,
Bringing to both my cheeks the blush of shame,
Proffered the healing balm; 'tis said the lance
Of Peleus that Achilles wielded well
Was likewise wont to hurt and after heal.   5

Turning our back upon the noisome trench
Once more we mounted its encircling ledge
And plodded on in silence. In the gloom
Of murky twilight, neither night nor day,
My vision hardly reached beyond my stride,   10
But suddenly a horn's deep-throated note
With mightier volume than a thunderclap
Broke on my ears and brought my startled eyes
To seek the quarter whence it issued forth.
Brave Roland on the field of Roncesvalles   15
When Charlemagne's knightly company was lost
Blew not a blast more terrible to hear.
Closely I peered ahead and seemed to see
The shadowy shapes of lofty towers rise
And asked, "What city's battlements are these?"   20
My master then: "Because you strain your sight,
Seeking to pierce too deeply through the fog,
Your concept wanders widely from the truth.
When closer we approach you may perceive
How senses cheat when objects are remote.   25
So onward; goad yourself to greater haste."
Relenting then, he gently took my hand
And added: "That you may not be alarmed
By the true nature of these monstrous forms
Learn that not towers but mighty giants loom   30
Before us; round the chasm's inner edge
They stand with nether half beneath the rim."

As, when a fog lifts slowly, figures vague
At first concealed beneath the misty veil
Become more sharply outlined to the eye,   35
So as we made our progress toward the pit
And penetrated the dark atmosphere
Illusion faded while my terror grew.
For, as above its garland of high walls
Montereggione lifts its towered crown,   40
So on the bank that girds the infernal well
With half their awesome bodies high upraised,
Were set the huge Earth Titans whom Jove still
With vengeance threatens from a thunderous sky.
One massive head already I discerned   45
With chest and shoulders and the upper paunch
And two great arms close hanging by the sides.
Nature in truth did well when she renounced
Creation of such monstrous living things
Who had been else such fearful slaves of Mars,   50
And if she still bears elephants and whales
He who will judge her with a subtle mind
Will find her here more just and more discreet;
For where the virtue of intelligence
Is added to malevolence and power   55
'Tis then no human recourse may avail.
In length and breadth the giant face recalled
The pine of bronze adorning Peter's Square,
And of like measure were the mammoth limbs.
The bank which like an apron hid the half   60
Beneath the waistline yet revealed above
Such towering bulk that no three men could reach,
Though they were tall as Frisians, to the hair.
I guessed a span of thirty full great palms
From shoulder down to where the cloak is pinned.   65

Yet very gently did he put us down.

Inferno XXXI, 139

"Raphel may amech zabi almi,"
The monster thundered down in syllables
Of uncouth speech appropriate to his tongue.
Then did my guide address him: "Doltish soul,
Blow on your horn and use it to relieve   70
Whatever wrath or passion stirs your breast.
Grope 'round your neck, there hangs the trumpet cord,
O clumsy fumbler; nay look well below
And see the horn itself against your chest."
Aside to me: "He gives himself away;   75
For this is Nimrod on whose mad account
No common speech remains to link mankind.
We'll pass him by nor waste our words in vain
For every language is to him as his
To other ears, incomprehensible."   80
Leftward we turned and walked a longer way
And at a bowshot's length we found his mate
Yet more enormous and of fiercer mien.
I know not who had bound him where he stood
But, one before and one behind his back,   85
Both hands were fettered and the length of chain
Went five times round his exposed upper part.
"This haughty Titan sought to test his strength
In trial with great Jove," my guide explained,
"Hence his reward. Ephialtes he is called;   90
His rash attempt was made when Titans rose
And made the gods to tremble. The stout arms
He plied so boldly then he moves no more."
I made request: "If it might be, I would
That my eyes might have sufferance to gaze   95
On ponderous Briareus." But he replied:
"Hard by Antaeus you will find unbound
And free to speak. 'Tis he will lower us

227

Down to the final depth of evil's source.
But he whom you would see stands far from here 100
Fettered like this one and quite similar
Save that his aspect is still more untamed."
Never did shock of earthquake rock a tower
With greater force than Ephialtes showed
Shaking himself, so more than ever yet 105
Death-fear I felt, and fear had brought me death
Had I not noticed his restraining bonds.

So we resumed our march and soon we neared
Antaeus' bulk which, not to count his head,
A full five ells emerged above the shelf. 110
"Earth son, who on the fateful valley floor,
Where Hannibal with routed cohorts fled
Leaving to Scipio fame's heritage,
Did once a thousand lions hunt and slay;
You of whose puissance such tales are told 115
That some, it seems, maintain the Sons of Earth
Would have achieved their triumph o'er the gods
Had you assisted in your brothers' war,
Do you – be not reluctant – set us down
On deep Cocytus locked in icy grip. 120
Bid us not go to Tityos nor Typhon;
What here is longed for, this man may bestow,
Wherefore bend down, turn not your snout aside.
He may yet grant you glory on the earth,
For he still lives and hopes for many years 125
Unless Grace summon him before his time."
So Virgil ended, and delaying not
The Titan, stretching forth his mighty hands,
Whose grasp of old was felt by Hercules,
Seized on my master. As he felt their clutch, 130

228

"Come, let me hold you here," he quickly called
And made one bundle of himself and me.
As Garisenda seems to one who stands
Beneath the slanting side and sees a cloud
Float overhead against the leaning peak   135
So seemed Antaeus as I, open-mouthed,
Watched him bend over. Such a sight it was
I well wished we had come another way.
Yet very gently did he put us down
Upon the icy bottom which engulfs   140
Judas and Lucifer, and, lingering not,
Snapped back again upright as a ship's mast.

CANTO XXXII

Their melting eyes dropped tears upon their cheeks,
Which, frozen by the cold, ice-cased their orbs.

Inferno XXXII, 47–48

Could I but find the crude and strident rhymes
Accordant with the lowest bleak abyss
On which Hell's rocky circles are sustained
I might the substance of my vision here
More graphically transcribe. I have them not   5
And here tread timidly. No idle game
For laughing pastime is it to depict
The center of our sinful universe,
Nor venture for the prattling tongues of babes.
Nay, but the Muses through whose virtue Thebes   10
Was by Amphion walled, may they avail
So here my telling turn not from the truth.

O hapless folk, of all most ill-conceived,
Even to speak of where you lie is hard;
Better for ye had ye been sheep or goats!   15

We stood within the deep well's darkest depth
Far down below the towering Titan's feet,
And I looked up and saw the wall rise steep
And heard one speak: "Take care how you tread here:
See that you strike not with your heedless stride   20
Your brothers' heads, sad wretches that we are."
At this I turned and saw I stood upon
A frozen lake far stretching in the gloom
And ice-bound to the semblance of smooth glass.
The Balkan Danube never cast a veil   25
Of such compacted cold upon its course,
Nor yet the Don beneath the Northern stars,
As here we saw; had lofty Tambernic
Or Pietrapiana crashed upon this floor
The shock would scarce have cracked the icy rim.   30
And much as frogs in pools thrust out their snouts

233

To voice their croaking in the summer eve
When farm girls dream of gleaning in the fields,
So here, all livid-hued, the sorry shades
Were fixed in ice, projecting only forth   35
So much of face as might betray their shame
With teeth a-chattering like beaks of storks.
Each one kept his bleak visage downward cast:
'Mongst them the jaws bear witness to the cold
And eyes attest the evilness of heart.   40

When my eyes had surveyed the wintry scene
I glanced beneath me: two stood at my feet
So closely linked their locks were intertwined.
Them I addressed: "You two so tightly locked
Together breast to breast, say who you are."   45
Throwing their heads back, they looked up at me;
Their melting eyes dropped tears upon their cheeks,
Which, frozen by the cold, ice-cased their orbs.
Never were wooden beams more closely bound
By tightened bolt than was this pair of souls;   50
So hateful was their coupling that like rams
In stubborn wrath they butted one another.
A third who stood close by with head still bent
(I marked the frost had shorn him of his ears),
Cried out: "Why peer so into our cold glass?   55
As for these two, know that Bisenzo flows
Where they and their sire Albert once held sway;
One mother bore them both; this lake of Cain
You might search over and discover none
More fitted to be fixed in gelatine.   60
Nay, not the traitorous soul whose breast and shade
Alike were pierced by Arthur's mighty thrust,
Nor yet Foccaccia nor this fellow here

234

My hand already held his curling locks
And more than one tuft I had reft from him.

Inferno XXXII, 102–103

Whose head obstructs me and cuts short my sight:
He bore the name of Sassol Mascheroni;   65
If you are Tuscan I need add no more.
As for myself, I'm Camición dei Pazzi,
Carlín I wait to palliate my guilt."
A thousand faces more I saw with cold
All dog-like, whence deep horror still I bear,   70
And always will, of frozen pools of ice.
And as we toward that midpoint onward moved
Which brings together every weighted mass
And I still shivered in the timeless shade,
Whether through destiny or chance or will   75
I know not but my foot struck 'gainst the face
Of one head of the many in our path.
In tears reproach was made: "Why tread on me?
If you come not to add your vengeful meed
For Montaperti, why this injury?"   80
"Master," I said then, "pray await me here
So that this shade may free me of a doubt.
And after I shall hasten as you bid."
My leader paused and I inquired of him
Who still cried out in curses bitterly: 85
"Who, pray, are you to chide your fellow thus?"
He answered: "Nay, say rather who you are
Who go through Antenora kicking folk;
Were you still living 'twere too much to bear."
"I live indeed," I answered him, "and dear   90
It may be to you; if you ask for fame
Your name with others I may register."
And he: "The opposite is my desire;
Take yourself off and trouble me no more;
Such flattering arts persuade not in this gulch."   95
I seized him by the hair around his nape

235

And said to him: "Now let me hear your name
Or I will peel each hair from off your skull."
But yet he cried: "Tear every hair away
And fall upon my head a thousand times   100
Yet who I am I'll not reveal to you."
My hand already held his curling locks
And more than one tuft I had reft from him
The while with downcast eyes he howled in pain
When came another voice: "What's wrong there, Bocca?   105
Is not the chattering of frozen jaws
Sufficient for you? Must you bark as well?
What devil has laid hold on you?" "Enough,"
I said, "I would not have you answer more,
Vile traitor; tidings I will bear of you   110
Veracious and redounding to your shame."
"Go then," he answered, "and tell what you will,
But if from here you issue do not fail
To tell of him who showed so prompt a tongue
And here bewails the silver of the French.   115
'I saw,' so you may say, 'Duera's knight
Down where the sinners are cooled off below.'
If you are asked of others you have seen
You have beside you him of Beccherìa
Whose neckpiece Florence slit. Yet further on   120
Lies Gian de' Soldanieri, near, I think,
To Ganelon and Tebaldello, who
Threw wide Faenza's gate while all men slept."

When we had moved some way apart from him
I saw two sinners ice-bound in one crack,   125
So one head seemed to be its fellow's hood;
And as 'neath hunger's spur bread is devoured
Even so the upper figure set his teeth

236

Into the other's brain above the nape.
And no more wolfishly did Tydeus gnaw   130
His adversary's temples in his rage
Than this one chewed the skull and other parts.
"You there, revealing in such bestial style
Your hatred against him whom you devour;
Tell me the cause thereof, with this accord: 135
That if with reason you complain of him,
Learning his sin and your identity
I may repay you in the world above
If my tongue withers not within my throat."

CANTO XXXIII

Raising his mouth up from his awful meal
The sinner wiped it clean upon the hairs
Of that head he had ravaged from behind
And then began: "You ask me to renew
Grief past despair that suffocates my heart   5
Even to think on ere I start to speak,
But if my words may be the seed of shame
For this ignoble traitor that I gnaw
Then you will see one speak and weep at once.
I know not who you are nor in what way   10
You have come down here, but a Florentine
In truth I think you when I hear your speech.
Learn that I was Count Ugolino called,
This fellow is the Archbishop Ruggieri;
Why I am such a neighbor I will show.   15
How by the working of his wicked plans
Trusting in him I first was cast in prison
And after killed there is no need to say;
But what you cannot yet have heard from men,
That is, the inhuman nature of my death,   20
Hear now and judge if he has done me ill.
A narrow opening in Starvation Mews –
So named for me, but destined to immure
Others to come – had filtered to my eyes
Already many moons when came the dream   25
That rent apart the veil of future ills.
This shade appeared as master of the hunt
Chasing the wolf and wolf cubs on the hill
Which cuts off Lucca from the Pisans' sight.
With lean hound-bitches, trained and keen to kill,   30
Gualandi with Sismondi and Lanfranchi
He had sent forth as leaders of the pack.
After a short run – so my dream revealed –

Both sire and sons were spent and I beheld
The cutting hound fangs lacerate their flanks.   35
When I awakened just before the dawn
I heard my children who were jailed with me
Sob in their sleep and whimper for their bread.
Cruel you must be if yet you feel no grief
Thinking on what my fearing heart foretold;   40
If here you weep not, what can bring you tears?
Now they awaken as the hour draws near
At which our rations had been brought to us
And each one trembled, mindful of his dream;
I heard below the gate swung to and locked   45
Beneath the dreadful tower, whence wordlessly
I looked upon the faces of my sons.
I wept not for I turned to stone within;
Tears sprang from them and little Anselm cried:
'What ails you, father, that you eye us so?'   50
Yet still I wept not and made no reply
Through that whole day and the successive night
Until the day dawned on the world anew.
Then when a feeble sun ray struggled in
To our sad prison showing to my sight   55
On four young faces my own aspect drawn
In bitter anguish I chewed both my hands
And they who thought my act revealed desire
Of nourishment, sprang up and quickly said:
'Father, our misery were much assuaged   60
If you partook of us; this fleshly dress
You clothed us in is yours to take again.'
Then I was still lest I increase their grief;
Mute were we all for that day and the next;
Say, rocky earth, why did you not split wide!   65
The fourth day came, and Gaddo at my feet

I wept not for I turned to stone within.

Inferno XXXIII, 48

Cast himself down and said: 'Have you no help
For me, O father?' With these words he died
And one by one, true as you see me here
I saw between the fifth day and the sixth   70
The three remaining fall before my eyes,
Whence, blinded now, I groped to feel their touch
And called their names in vain for two more days.
Till hunger over grief at last prevailed."

When he had told his tale with sidelong glance   75
He fell again upon the wretched skull
With teeth as hard as hound's teeth on the bone.
Ah Pisa, shameful byword of all men
Of that fair country wherein "sì" is heard,
Since vengeance at your neighbors' hands is slow   80
May your Gorgona and Capraia move
And hedge the Arno where it joins the sea
So it may drown all souls within your walls.
What though Count Ugolino had the blame
Of having tricked you of the forts by guile,   85
Yet should you not have tortured so his sons.
Their tender youth affirmed the innocence,
O modern Thebes, of Uguccione and
Brigata and the brothers named above.

Onward we went to where the frozen crust   90
Holds in its grip another style of folk
Not downthrust these but heads thrown back reversed.
Here tears themselves allow no room for tears
And grief thus barred from outlet through the eyes
Turns back within to multiply their pain;   95
The first tears block the eyes and, as beneath
A crystal visor, all the eye-well fills.

243

And though as it were calloused by the cold
Perceptive sense had all but left my face
Yet did I seem to feel a chilling blast,   100
Wherefore I asked: "Master, who moves this wind?
Are not all vaporous currents stilled down here?"
He answered me: "Soon will you come to where
Your eye will give reply to what you ask,
Seeing the sorry cause of this stirred air."   105
Hereat a wretch fixed in the hard ice block
Called out to us: "O souls so inhumane
As to deserve the lowest place of all,
Remove these rigid veilings from my eyes;
Let me pour out the grief that packs my heart   110
A little ere the tears freeze tight again."
And I to him: "If you would have my aid
Say who you are; if I relieve you not
May I descend deep in the icy depths."
"Fra Alberigo I am called," he said,   115
"Whose orchard of ill will produced such fruit
As to repay me here dates for each fig."
"Already are you dead?" I asked of him,
And he replied: "How fares my body now
On earth above I know not, for this ring   120
Of Ptolomaea has such privilege
That often hither falls the sinner's soul
Ere Atropos has cut the thread of life.
And that you may more readily remove
The frozen tears that choke my grief-filled eyes,   125
Know that immediately a soul betrays
As I did then, a demon occupies
The body, guiding it thenceforth until
The course appointed for its life is run.
The soul itself down to this cistern rains.   130

244

He fell again upon the wretched skull.

Inferno xxxiii, 76

Indeed it may be that the flesh still lives
Of him whose shade is wintering close by me.
This you must know if you are newly come
For he is Branca d'Oria; for some years
He has been thus imprisoned." "Now," I said,   135
"I think you would deceive me, for I know
Ser Branca has not yet come to his death
But eats and drinks and sleeps and puts on clothes."
"Not yet had Michael Zanche been immersed,"
He answered, "in the Badpaws' trench above   140
Wherein the glutinous pitch forever boils
When this soul left a devil in his place
Within his body; likewise did his kinsman,
Who in his treachery abetted him.
And now extend your hand this way," he begged,   145
"And cleanse my eyes." But I did not do so
And villainy to him was courtesy.
Ah Genoese, ah race of men divorced
From all good customs, filled with every vice,
Say why does earth not sweep you from her face?   150
A citizen of yours I found among
Romagna's basest souls, of such vile works
That while his flesh still seems to live above,
The soul Cocytus bathes in its bleak flood.

CANTO XXXIV

"*Vexilla regis prodeunt inferni*
Outspread toward us, look forward now and see,"
My master bade, "if they may be descried."
As when in heavy fog the earth is veiled
Or when night's darkness shrouds our hemisphere   5
A mill appears with sails stirred by the wind,
So here a like shape seemed to meet my eye,
And whipped at by the gale I drew myself
The closer to my guide, my only shield.
Now we were come where all the sinners lay   10
(I shudder as I shape the tale in verse)
All ice-encased like bits of straw in glass
Some with head upright, others lying prone,
Some cast face downwards, others curled supine.

Onward we strode until my master chose   15
To show me that dread creature, once so fair.
He bade me halt and moved a step ahead
Saying: "Lo, there stands Dis; here is the pass
Where you must summon all your fortitude."
How chilled and weak, O reader, I became,   20
Ask me not here for I could not transcribe
However faintly half the fear I felt.
I lived no longer, neither did I die;
Imagine, if your fancy may avail,
What state was mine, a living death in life.   25
The sovereign of evil's dolorous realm
From chest to head loomed up above the ice
And I am closer to a giant's size
Than giants' stature measures 'gainst his arms.
By this proportion reckon what must be   30
The fearsome bulk of such a monstrous fiend.
If once he was as fair as now he's foul

249

And yet raised jealous against his Lord,
Then rightly is he source of every woe.
A wondrous thing it was to see his head,   35
Wearing three faces, scarlet to the fore;
The other two, united with the first
Sprang from between the shoulders and were joined
Above to form his crest. The right in hue
Was whitish yellow, on the left his shade   40
Was such to look upon as is the tint
Of those who dwell beside the Afric Nile.
Beneath each head two mighty wings emerged
In due proportion to the monster's bulk,
And sails I never saw of such expanse.   45
No feathers did they bear but like a bat's
Their covering was; incessantly they flapped
And raised three winds that steady blew and chill,
Holding Cocytus ever bound in ice.
Six giant eyes dripped tears which on three chins   50
Commingled with the blood-bespattered drool.
In each mouth Satan mangled with his teeth
A sinner, each jaw moving like a brake
So that three wretches anguished as he chewed.
He of the front mouth less from biting writhed   55
Than from the flaying of the angry claws;
His back was stripped and stripped again of flesh.
"Yon soul above who suffers greatest pain
Is Judas," so my master's voice affirmed,
"With head thrust in and legs a-dangling free;   60
Brutus it is who hangs from the black jowls
(See how he squirms about in silent pain);
The third is Cassius, large and heavyset.
But come, night rises once again and we
Must take our leave. Now we've seen every thing."   65

A wondrous thing it was to see his head,
Wearing three faces.

Inferno xxxiv, 35–36

As he commanded round his neck I cast
My arms, and, choosing proper time and place,
The while the baleful wings were wide outspread,
He took firm grip upon the hairy ribs
Then climbed straight down from tuft to furry tuft   70
Between the frozen ice pack and the pelt.

When we had reached the point whereat the thigh
Begins its swelling curve to meet the haunch
My leader with much effort and great strain
Turned him about to place his head where first   75
His feet had been and clung fast to the fur,
As one who upward climbs, so that my thought
Was that we made our way towards Hell again.
"Be heedful here and mark that by such stairs
We must from such great evil take our leave,"   80
My master warned and panted with fatigue.
Then through a rocky crevice he came forth
And seating me upon the rim he sprang
With agile leap and rested by my side.
I raised my eyes and thought to see again   85
As I had left him, Lucifer upright,
But saw instead his legs projecting forth;
And what confusion did I suffer then
Let dolts imagine who may not conceive
What point it was that we had left behind.   90

"Arise and walk," my master ordered me,
"Long is the journey and the road is rough;
The sun already moves halfway through tierce."
No palace hall it was wherein we stood
But a natural grotto carved out in the rock   95
With stone-hard flooring and but little light.

251

"Before I wrench myself from this abyss,"
I asked of Virgil as I stood to go,
"Deliver me from error and disclose
Where is the ice? And why does Satan stand   100
Reversed? And how in such a sudden time
Has the sun moved from night to early morn?"
And he to me: "You fancy we are yet
Yon side of center where I seized the pelt
Of that dread dragon who divides the earth.   105
On that side were we while I yet climbed down
But when I turned then did you pass the point
Whither from every hand all weights are drawn,
Now we have come into the hemisphere
Opposite to the one by land bedecked   110
Under whose zenith died the Man divine
Whose birth and life were innocent of sin.
Now do your feet stand in the little sphere
That forms the other facet of Judecca;
Here it is morn when yonder evening falls;   115
This creature whose fur-clumps gave us our stair
Is still fixed tightly as he was before.
On this side did he fall from out the skies:
For fear of him the land which erst was here
Withdrew and, wrapped beneath its ocean veil,   120
Flew to our hemisphere; it may be too
The earthstuff on this side left this spot void
In flight from him, and to the surface rose."

A place there is below as far remote
From Beelzebub as his tomb's height extends.   125
Unknown to sight, its presence is revealed
By trickling of a stream that here descends
Through a rock channel that its waters' flow

Has worn, and, swerving little from the straight,
Over that hidden way my lord and I   130
Made entrance, seeking once more to return
Up to the world of light. Onward we climbed,
He first, I second, stopping not to rest
Until at last through fissured earth I spied
The jeweled loveliness that Heaven wears   135
And we came forth once more to see the stars.

NOTES

CANTO I

1-2] The opening line dates the action of the poem. "Three score and ten" being the normal life span, Dante (1265-1321) tells us that he is thirty-five years old: it is therefore 1300. He "finds himself" in the wood on Maundy Thursday, April 7 of that year (Moore, *Studies* III, 144 ff.), or "more probably" March 24 (Sapegno and Chimenz). Good Friday of 1300, the day on which Dante actually begins his journey, fell on April 8. But the "historical" anniversary of the Crucifixion, according to mediaeval reckoning, was the twenty-fifth of March, the day also of the Incarnation and, it was thought, of the Creation of Adam (see lines 38-39). It is also very close to the spring equinox and, we may add, was New Year's Day in mediaeval Florence. . . . As for Dante's midpoint, cf. Isaiah 38: 10.

13-16] Remo Fasani (*Il poema sacro* [Florence: 1964]) suggests that the "hill," "vale" and "star" are a kind of prefiguring of the realms Dante is to visit, Purgatory, Hell and Heaven. The "star" here is the sun; allegorically divine grace.

29] A rather baffling line. According to Boccaccio (followed by Sapegno and many others), simply a way of saying that the poet is moving up hill. For an ingenious modern exegesis see John Freccero, "Dante's Firm Foot and the Journey without a Guide," *Harvard Theological Review*, Vol. LII (1959), pp. 245-81.

31-47] The three beasts, suggested by Jeremiah 5: 6, were identified by the older commentators as symbolizing respectively Lust, Violence and Avarice. Some moderns have other interpretations: for Fraticelli, for example, the animals would represent Envy, Pride and Avarice (following Ciacco's dictum in Canto VI, line 73) and carry as well the political meanings of Florence (spotted because of the black and white rivalry), France and the Roman Curia. Others see in them a prefiguring of the three great divisions of Hell: Incontinence, Violence and Fraud.

67-68] Virgil was born in 70 B.C.; Caesar died in 44 B.C.

70-1] Anchises was the father of Aeneas.

76] *Virgil*: traditionally in the allegory Virgil stands for human reason. He also has wider associations: Charles Williams, for example, finds in him "at least four significances: he is Virgil, and poetry, and Philosophy, and the Institution or the City," (*The Figure of Beatrice* [London: 1943], p. 70). He also at times seems to speak for ancient learning and the Roman Tradition and now and again for Imperialism. For another reason too he is a well-chosen guide for this sort of journey: the middle ages held him to be a sorcerer. On the relations of Dante and Virgil see J. H. Whitfield, *Dante and Virgil* (Oxford: 1949).

84] Probably Dante refers here to his moral odes, written in lofty style (Sapegno, Chimenz).

97] *Greyhound*: some deliverer Dante hopes for. Possibly Can Grande della Scala (see *Paradise* XVII, 76-78). Other suggestions have been varied: an Emperor (Henry VII?), Christ in his second coming, even the poet himself. See L. Olschki, *The Myth of Felt* (Los Angeles: 1949). The problem is complicated by its inevitable association with the DXV of *Purgatory* XXXIII, 43.

100] *two Feltros*: perhaps meaning between Feltre (near Venice) and Montefeltro (Romagna); this would suit those who believe Can Grande is meant. But the phrase may mean simply "between felt and felt," i. e. swaddled in coarse cloth, which is to say of humble birth: some of the old commentators suggest this.

102-103] *Camilla*, etc.: characters in the *Aeneid*, slain in the war between Trojans and Latins.

108-17] These lines contain a kind of prospectus of the journey, outlining the functions of the successive realms.

111] The second death is that of the soul.

116] The reference is to Beatrice.

CANTO II

13] *Silvio's sire*: Aeneas, of *Aeneid* VI.

26] St. Paul (see II Cor. 12: 2-4).

65] *Beatrice*: Dante's youthful love, celebrated in the *Vita Nuova*. Daughter of Folco Portinari, married Simon de' Bardi; died 1290 (Boccaccio).

70-72] The "smallest sphere" is that of the moon: Beatrice causes mankind to surpass all else on earth. A courtly speech, addressed to a beautiful and compassionate woman. Perhaps we are here to think of Beatrice in her allegorical aspect of Theology, or simply human virtue (Sapegno). In the *Vita Nuova* (x, 2) Dante speaks of her as "queen of the virtues."

84-85] The blessed cannot be moved by the torments of Hell. (See *Purgatory* I, 89-91.)

86] *Lady*: the Virgin Mary.

89] *Lucia*: St. Lucy, patroness of vision, here allegorically illuminating grace.

93] Rachel represents the contemplative life.

99] There has been no stream mentioned in the narrative. Does the poet wish us to think of Acheron, soon to be reached and marking the frontier of true Hell? (Benvenuto and others.) More probably, in the opinion of most commentators, it is simply metaphorical language to signify our turbulent and sin-ridden mortal life, compared to which the death of the body is less to be feared. The image was perhaps suggested, consciously or otherwise, by the figure of I, 20-22.

CANTO III

5-7] Power, Wisdom and Love, the attributes of the Trinity in the respective persons of Father, Son and Holy Ghost. Cf. *Paradise Lost*, VII, 192-96: "Meanwhile the Son / On his great expedition now appeared, / Girt with omnipotence, with radiance crowned / Of majesty divine, sapience and love / Immense, and all his Father in him shone."

19 ff.] The vestibule is Dante's own invention, at least in terms of Christian eschatology; its literary source is the *vestibulum Orci* of *Aeneid* VI.

59] The oldest commentators agree in identifying this individual as the Pope Celestinus V, who abdicated after only a few months in office (1294), thus making way for the election of Boniface VIII, Dante's enemy. The good reputation that Celestinus enjoyed and the fact that he was canonized in 1313 have led later scholars to suggest other identifications for the figure alluded to here. Benvenuto suggested Esau; other candidates include Pontius Pilate, Diocletian and such Florentine leaders as Gian della Bella and Vieri de' Cerchi.

81] *ancient oarsman*: Charon, legendary ferryman of the Styx (see *Aeneid* VI, 298-300).

90] Charon alludes to the bark which bears the souls of the saved from Tibermouth to the shores of Purgatory (see *Purgatory* II, 99).

CANTO IV

15] This line is suggestively echoed by XXXIV, 133.

52] Virgil died in 19 B.C. The deliverance of the Patriarchs (the Harrowing of Hell) took place when Christ descended into Limbo after the Crucifixion.

88] *the satirist*: it would seem that Dante was not familiar with the *Odes* and *Epodes* and knew of Horace only the *Ars Poetica* (Moore, *op. cit.*, I, 197; who also points out how the company of poets here is identical with the group in the *Vita Nuova* XXV). Horace would not have been offended at being described as a satirist; he so defines himself in *Ars Poetica*, 235 (Grandgent). With regard to the other poets of this supreme hierarchy we may add that Dante apparently knew of Homer only a few fragmentary quotations at second hand, was quite familiar with the material of the *Metamorphoses* of Ovid, which he may have got from mediaeval summaries rather than from the original (see C. A. Robson, "Dante's Use in the *Divina Commedia* of the Mediaeval Allegories on Ovid," in *Centenary Essays on Dante* [Oxford: 1965]) and shared the mediaeval admiration for Lucan, author of the *Pharsalia*, to whom he turned frequently for historical data (Moore, *op. cit.*, p. 228).

104] The castle stands for human wisdom or achievement. The seven walls symbolize the four moral virtues (prudence, temperance, fortitude and justice) and the three intellectual virtues, (understanding, knowledge and wisdom); the gates represent liberal arts of the *trivium* (grammar, logic and rhetoric) and the *quadrivium* (music, arithmetic, geometry, astronomy); the stream stands for eloquence. So Grandgent and many commentators. There are other interpretations; see for example J. B. Fletcher, "Dante's School of the Eagle," *Romanic Review*, XXII, 191.

119] *Electra*: mother of Dardanus, the founder of Troy (*Aeneid* VIII, 134-35).

122] *Camilla*: warrior virgin of the Latins; see I, 100 (*Aeneid* XI, 498 ff).
Penthesilea: Queen of the Amazons (*Aeneid* I, 490 ff).

123] *Latinus*: King of Latium, father of Lavinia who married Aeneas (*Aeneid* VII, 45 ff).

126] *Lucretia*: wife of Lucius Tarquinius Collatinus; having been violated by Sextus Tarquinius, she committed suicide. Her act encouraged a revolt against the royal house of the Tarquins and resulted in the establishment of the Roman Republic, 510 B.C.
Julia: Caesar's daughter, wife of Pompey.
Marcia: wife of Cato of Utica (see *Purgatory* I, 80).
Cornelia: the mother of the Gracchi.

127] *Saladin*: the famous leader of the Saracens, opponent of Richard Coeur de Lion (1137?-93).

134] *Democritus*: originator of the "atomic theory": Dante knew of him only through Cicero; likewise secondhand is his acquaintance with the other Greek Philosophers herein enumerated; the theory of Empedocles to which Dante alludes in XII, 37-38, he probably got through Aristotle. This whole passage is a kind of brief résumé of the history of philosophy Dante gives us in the fourth book of the *Convivio*.

138] *Dioscorides*: Greek physician of first century A.D., wrote a treatise on plants and their mediaeval qualities.

139] *Tully*: Cicero, whose prose works (though not his orations) were well known to Dante. See Moore, *op. cit.*, pp. 258-73.
Linus: a legendary Greek poet. "Seneca moralist" was thought to be a different person from the dramatist.

140] *Euclid*: the famous geometer of Athens, lived about 300 B.C.
Ptolemy: the great astronomer of Alexandria, second century B.C. Designer of Dante's cosmos.

141] *Avicenna*: (Ibn-Sina, 980-1037) Arab philosopher and physician; here associated with the great physicians of the Western tradition, Hippocrates of the fifth century B.C. and Galen of the second century A.D.

142] *Averroes*: twelfth century Spanish Moor, celebrated for his scholarship. His "great commentary" on Aristotle was used by St. Thomas Aquinas; "Averroism" became known as a liberal, sometimes heretical, current in mediaeval philosophy.

CANTO V

4] *Minos*: one of the three judges of the Underworld (see *Aeneid* VI, 432-33).

34] The cleft or fissure in the rocky wall is the mark of the earthquake that took place after the Crucifixion (see Canto XXI, 106-108). Here it serves to remind the sinners of the salvation they have lost.

55] *Semiramis*: Queen of Assyria.

59-60] Dido, widow of Sichaeus, deserted by Aeneas (see *Aeneid* IV).

63] Achilles fell in love with the Trojan Princess Polyxena and was slain by her brother Paris, according to mediaeval accounts.

71] *those two*: Francesca da Rimini, daughter of Guido Vecchio da Polenta, married (1275) Gianciotto, son of Malatesta da Verrucchio, Lord of Rimini, and her brother-in-law, Paolo. There is no really historical evidence for the episode which Dante narrates.

94] *The town*: Ravenna.

99] Because she was killed with no time for repentance.

104] Gianciotto, having treacherously slain the lovers, will, after his death, find his place in the lowest division of Hell, among other traitors to kinsmen. It has been suggested, most recently by Donadoni ("Tre donne della *Commedia*," in *Discorsi letterari* [Palermo: 1905]) that this line is spoken not by Francesca but by Paolo.

119] *your teacher*: Virgil.

133] *Gallehaut*: the page who carried messages between Launcelot and Guinevere; hence a general term for a go-between.

CANTO VI

12] *Cerberus*: guardian of the lower world (see *Aeneid* VI, 417 ff.).

49] *serene*: so mortal life seems to the damned. The saved have another point of view.

50] *Ciacco*: it is not certain who the historical Ciacco was. Some have identified him as the poet Ciacco dell'Anguillaia but it is mere conjecture. "Ciacco," according to Buti, is a nickname meaning "pig" – but again, it is probably also a proper name in its own right, deriving from Giacomo (Chimenz).

63] *the rural party*: the Whites, so called because headed by the Cerchi, who had come into Florence from the country. The reference here is to the skirmish of May 1300, as a result of which the Blacks were exiled.

64-67] By 1302, aided by Charles of Valois and the Pope, the Blacks were back in power and many Whites were exiled.
him who straddles (piaggia): Boniface, whose conduct in 1300 was ambiguous.

68] *for long*: because they are still in power when Dante writes these lines Ciacco cannot be precise.

71] *Two just men*: some critics think that here "two" is not a specific number but merely a general expression meaning "a few." But the language implies that Dante must have had his pair clearly in mind. If so, then certainly he is one of them and Guido Cavalcanti seems a likely candidate for the other (Gmelin).

77-78] We shall find Farinata degli Uberti among the heretics, Canto X; Tegghiaio Aldobrandi and Jacopo Rusticucci appear in Canto XVI with Guido Guerra; Mosca de' Lamberti is one of the sowers of discord (Canto XXVIII). We shall hear nothing more of the unidentified Arrigo.

93-94] Judgment Day.

104] *Science*: Aristotelian philosophy; "the general concept here expressed is Aristotelian" (Chimenz). Torraca also cites St. Thomas.

113] *Plutus*: ancient god of wealth. Dante's Italian is "Pluto" which may signify Pluto, king of the underworld. The commentators are uncertain as to which of these legendary characters Dante had in mind: he may not have known of the distinction himself since even in antiquity they were frequently confused (Toynbee).

CANTO VII

1] Translatable perhaps as "Oh Satan, oh Satan, God!" or "Oh Satan, oh Satan, alas!" (Chimenz). Or it may be meant "to produce the effect of unintelligible jargon" (Grandgent).

10] The triumph of the archangel Michael over Lucifer and his rebels (Apoc. 12:7 ff.) is here recalled as an example of the power of the omnipotent before which Plutus must yield.

21] *Charybdis*: in the Strait of Messina (see *Aeneid* III, 420-23).

66 ff.] Dante's idea of Fortune owes much to Boethius, Albertus Magnus and others but he is the first to accord her angelic status. On the subject see V. Cioffari, *The Conception of Fortune and Fate in the Works of Dante* (Cambridge, Mass.: 1940).

98] The stars that were rising in the East when Virgil responded to Beatrice's appeal have crossed the meridian and begun their descent. In other words it is past midnight and we are in the early morning of Easter Saturday.

108] Virgil too speaks of the "Stygian swamp" (*Aeneid* VI, 323).

110 ff.] Aristotle (*Ethics* IV, v), later followed by St. Thomas, described three classes of the wrathful, the *acuti*, the *amari* and the *difficiles* – respectively, in Grandgent's terminology, the "quick-tempered," the "sullen" and the "vindictive." Here there are two divisions, those on the surface and the submerged. Are both latter groups among the submerged? (It seems clear that those on the surface are the *acuti*.) Judging by their description it seems likely that only the *amari* are below the surface (Momigliano); the *difficiles* possibly elsewhere (Flamini).

CANTO VIII

18] *Phlegyas*: in Greek mythology a son of Mars who set fire to the temple of Delphi in revenge for the seduction of his daughter by Apollo. (*Aeneid* VI, 618-20; *Thebaid* I, 713 ff.)

60] *Filippo Argenti*: Filippo de' Cavicciuli, a branch of the Adimari family, called "Argenti" (silver) because it is said that he had his horses shod with that metal (Boccaccio). He seems to have been a personal enemy of Dante; the commentators (who all write after the fact) are not in agreement as to the source of this hostility. In *Paradise* XVI, 116, Dante again expresses his contempt for the Adimari clan.

80-81] *those . . . rejected*: the fallen angels.

95] *seven times*: here merely to indicate a general number: the phrase means simply "often." A Biblical usage; cf. Proverbs 24:16, Luke 7:2, etc.

121-23] A reference to the Harrowing of Hell.

CANTO IX

17] *first ring*: Limbo.

23] *Erichtho*: a sorceress, who, according to Lucan (*Pharsalia* II, 508-830) called up the spirit of a dead soldier to foretell the outcome of the war between Caesar and Pompey. Virgil's mission is Dante's own invention. One may note that the sibyl had given Aeneas similar comfort (*Aeneid* VI, 562-65).

53] *Medusa*: the Gorgon of classical mythology. It seems likely that the Furies in this allegory stand for the remorse of a guilty conscience and Medusa for the ultimate despair of forgiveness, which would be death to the soul. In such straits the Christian has need not only of Reason (Virgil), but eventually Grace (the divine messenger). Others see Medusa as heresy, sensuality (Boccaccio) or terror.

56] Theseus attempting to carry off Proserpine from Hades, was detained by the Infernal powers but later (according to one version of the myth) was rescued by Hercules (*Aeneid* VI, 392 ff.).

101] Hercules dragged Cerberus from Hades to the upper world, injuring him in the process (*Aeneid, loc. cit.*).

114] The field of Alischans near Arles was covered with tombs, thought to be those of Christian soldiers slain in battle with the Saracens.

115] *Pola*: now part of Jugoslavia and known as Pula; a city on the Istrian peninsula, in the environs of which was situated a similar cemetery. The gulf of Quarnero at the head of the Adriatic separates Istria from Dalmatia.

CANTO X

11] *Jehoshaphat*: the valley where the Last Judgment will be heard (see Joel 3: 2).

13] *Epicurus*: Greek philosopher (432-270 B.C.).

31] This is Farinata degli Uberti (died 1264), celebrated Florentine statesman and soldier; leader of the Ghibelline faction which routed the Guelphs at Montaperti in the valley of the Arbia (1260). See Canto VI, 77. On this episode see E. Auerbach, "Farinata and Cavalcante" in *Mimesis* (Anchor Edition, Garden City), pp. 151-76.

45] *twice*: in 1248 and 1260.

46] The Guelphs returned from their first exile in 1251 after the death of Frederick II (see line 114) and from their second in 1266, after the defeat of Manfred Benevento. Florence subsequently remained a Guelph city, hence Dante's taunt.

49] *another*: Cavalcante de' Cavalcanti.

57] *my son*: the famous Guido Cavalcanti (*circa* 1255-1300, but died after the ideal date of Dante's journey), Dante's "first friend" and fellow poet.

59-61] A controversial passage. Dante's grammar is ambiguous and may be literally translated either: "he who waits there guides me through here, (one) whom Guido perhaps scorned" or "he who waits there guides me through here perhaps to one whom Guido scorned." In the first version the reference would clearly be to Virgil, the clause "*forse . . . disdegno*" being in apposition with "*colui.*" In the second version some recent commentators (Sapegno and Chimenz among others) maintain that the reference is to Beatrice to whom in fact Virgil is leading the poet. The first interpretation seems to me more acceptable: it is the one given by all of the old commentators. I am inclined to agree with Gmelin who finds the second one "hardly tenable grammatically and even less so from the point of view of meaning." As to why Guido "held Virgil in scorn" there are a number of possibilities. Perhaps he was not an admirer, as Dante was, of classical literature; perhaps he did not share Dante's devotion to the Empire; perhaps he simply did not care for Virgil's poetry. Boccaccio says that Guido preferred philosophy to poetry and so scorned all poets including Virgil. Scartazzini cites the arguments of all the ancient commentators.

62-63] I. e. the reference to Guido and his presence among the heretics revealed him as the elder Cavalcanti.

77-78] Before fifty months have passed Dante too will know the bitterness of exile. He was exiled in January 1302; his hope of early return was frustrated by the failure of negotiations in 1304. The queen regnant in Hell is Hecate, in classical mythology also the moon goddess.

81-82] With the return of the Guelphs, the Uberti were banished from Florence, a sentence renewed in 1280 when many other Ghibellines were allowed to return.

84] See line 31, note.

89-90] At the Diet of Empoli, following the victory of Montaperti, the Ghibelline leaders considered razing Florence (see Villani, VI, 81).

117] Frederick II (1194-1250), King of Sicily and Emperor, whose emancipated court and style of living as well as his political hostility to the papacy caused him to be regarded as a heretic. The Cardinal is Ottaviano degli Ubaldini (*circa* 1210-73) also suspected of being an Epicurean.

128] *one*: Beatrice, whom Dante will meet in the terrestrial paradise on the summit of the mount of Purgatory. Actually it is from Cacciaguida (*Paradise* XVII) that Dante will learn of his destiny.

CANTO XI

8-9] *Anastasius* II: pope (496-98), whom Dante's authorities erroneously supposed had been led by *Photinus*, a deacon of Thessalonica, into heresy. Confused possibly with his contemporary, the Emperor Anastasius I (Toynbee).

22] *malice* (*malizia*): here in the sense of bad action; in line 82 it has a more restricted meaning, defining the category of violence.

24] *force or fraud*: it seems clear that here Dante had in mind the *vis* and *fraus* of Cicero's *De Officiis* I.

45] I. e., instead of being in Heaven where he would have been but for his sin.

50] *Sodom*: the wicked city of old: see Genesis 19.
Cahors: a city of southern France notorious for its usurers. The cities are symbols of the sins, both "unnatural."

70-72] Dante refers to the wrathful, the lustful, the gluttonous and the avaricious-prodigal group.

79] In *Ethics* VII Aristotle speaks of three categories of evil: malice, incontinence and bestiality. This is the source of Dante's three divisions of Hell, though his definitions do not exactly correspond to what Aristotle had in mind. See Kenelm Foster, "The Theology of the Inferno," in *God's Tree* (Westminster: 1957).

101] The testament is found in Aristotle's *Physics* II, II. The figure of human industry as God's grandchild is Dante's.

107] "In the sweat of thy face shalt thou eat bread" (Gen. 3: 19).

109-11] I. e., the usurer follows neither the law of nature nor that of its "follower," human industry.

113-14] From the position of the constellations (Pisces, on the horizon, and Ursa Major, now lying in the northwest, the quarter of the wind Caurus) we can calculate that it is about two hours before sunrise.

CANTO XII

4-5] Probably the Slavini di Marco, a land-slip near Rovereto between Trent and Verona on the left bank of the Adige, mentioned also by Albertus Magnus (Chimenz).

11-12] A reference to the Minotaur, the monster born of Pasiphae, queen of Crete, and a bull. The legend relates that the queen made use of a wooden cow to deceive the beast (see *Purgatory* XXVI, 40-41).

15-18] *Duke*: Theseus, who slew the Minotaur; he was aided by Ariadne, half sister of the monster.

33] Another reference to the earthquake that took place at the time of the Crucifixion (see Canto V, 35).

37] *those*: Empedocles and his followers, who held that the separation of the elements caused by hate makes the world possible; when the elements under the influence of love intermingle, chaos ensues.

40] *elsewhere*: see, for example, Canto V, 35.

51 ff.] The centaurs, half-man, half-horse, are suitable symbols of bestial violence. All mentioned here are notable figures in classical mythology. Chiron was the tutor of the young Achilles. Pholus attempted to break up the wedding of Pirothous and Hippodamia, thus causing strife and bloodshed. It was the poisoned shirt of Nessus that Dejanira gave to Hercules, believing it would revive his love for her; instead it drove him to madness and death (see Ovid, *Metamorphoses* IX).

103] Alexander the Great? More likely Alexander of Pherae in Thessaly (4th century B.C.). Both Cicero (*De officiis* II, VII, 13) and Brunetto Latini (*Tresor* II, CXIX, 6) cite this pair as examples of cruel tyrants (Chimenz).

104] *Dionysius*: tyrant of Syracuse (5th century B.C.).

107-108] Azzolino da Romano (1194-1259; see *Paradise* IX, 28) and Opizzo II d'Este (died 1293) were petty tyrants of Northern Italy, the former of the March of Treviso, the latter of Ferrara.

109] There were various versions, it would seem, of the death of Opizzo.

115] Guy de Montfort murdered Henry of Cornwall, nephew of Henry III of England, in a church in Viterbo (1271). Henry's heart was preserved in a golden vessel and placed on a column in London.

129] *Attila*: leader of the Huns, "the scourge of God," (406?-53).

130] *Pyrrhus*: probably Dante refers here to the son of Achilles who played such a violent role in the sack of Troy, killing Priam and one of his sons (*Aeneid* II, 526-558). *Sextus* (Pompeius): the piratical son of Pompey the Great (*Pharsalia* VI, 113 ff.).

131] Rinieri Pazzo and Rinieri da Corneto highwaymen, contemporaries of Dante.

CANTO XIII

7] Between Cécina and Corneto, in Tuscany, lies the wild and desolate region known as the Maremma.

11] See *Aeneid* III, 209 ff. for this episode.

45] There is a similar scene in the *Aeneid* (III, 22 ff.) in which the soul of the Trojan Prince Polydorus speaks through a tree.

56] The speaker is Pier delle Vigne (*ca.* 1190-1249), Chancellor of the Two Sicilies under Frederick II (see note to Canto X, line 117). In 1247 he fell into disgrace and subsequently committed suicide. He was not only a statesman but also a celebrated poet of the so-called "Sicilian School." Inspired by the Provençal troubadours, these early Italian poets wrote in a somewhat artificial style, full of verbal conceits. Dante echoes their style in this canto, thus paying a graceful tribute to his predecessors.

62] *That courtesan*: Envy.

76] Pier had been accused of conspiring against his master.

112] The fugitives are Jacopo da Sant'Andrea of Padua and Ercolano (Lano) of Siena. Both were notorious spendthrifts. Lano was killed in a battle fought at Pieve del Toppo, between Sienese and Aretines (1287).

140 ff.] In pagan days Mars was the patron of Florence. When Christianity came, St. John the Baptist was chosen patron saint of the town. The ancient statue of Mars was still preserved, however, and, after the razing of the city by Attila (A.D. 450) it was again set up on the Ponte Vecchio – or at least so Dante believed (see Villani, III, I). Actually Attila did not come near Florence and Totila, with whom the Hun was later confused, only besieged the town.

146] The speaker has been variously identified by the ancient commentators. Some suggest the jurist Lotto degli Agli; others the wealthy Rocco de' Mozzi. Benvenuto thought that it could be applied to any one of various Florentines who had committed suicide in this way. Boccaccio also says that there were many such suicides; he adds that Dante may have suppressed the name out of regard for the relatives.

CANTO XIV

15] In his campaign as leader of Pompey's army, Cato marched across the Libyan desert (see *Pharsalia* IX, 411 ff.).

20-22] Respectively the blasphemers, the usurers and the sodomites, although Dante does not meet them precisely in this order.

30] The incident is described in a letter from Alexander to Aristotle, now known to be false, but accepted in the Middle Ages. Dante had read a garbled version of this letter, apparently in Albertus Magnus, *De Meteoris*.

49] Capaneus during the siege of Thebes defied the gods and was slain by a bolt from Jove (*Thebaid* x).

53] *Mongibello*: Mt. Etna, the volcano in Sicily under which, according to legend, Vulcan and the Cyclopes forged the thunderbolts of Jove.

56] *Phlegra*: battle between the Titans and the gods.

76] *Bulicame*: a hot spring of red and sulphurous water, near Viterbo. Prostitutes were restricted to one of the streams flowing from it. G. Mazzoni (followed by Sapegno) reads *pectatrici* (hemp-combers) instead of *peccatrici* (sinful women) and explains the passage somewhat differently.

83-84] It is not immediately clear, in terms of the narrative, why the stream here is more worthy of remark than any of the others that Dante has already seen; both Acheron and Phlegethon also derive from the fissure in the old man of Crete. Perhaps one must seek an explanation in the allegory. "Does the quenching of the fire by boiling blood signify the appeasing of God's anger by human suffering? A symbol of atonement is manifestly out of place in the literal Hell; but allegorically Dante's lower world stands for the sinful life of man." (Grandgent.)

95] *Rhea*: mother of Jove. Saturn, his father, had vowed to devour his children, for it had been foretold that his son would dethrone him. Rhea had to conceal the child.

98 ff.] The old man of Crete, whose source is probably in Daniel 2: 32-33, is an allegory of the history of humanity. Damiata represents the East, the civilization of the past superseded by Rome, the West. The old man stands in Crete probably because Crete is thought of as the cradle of the Trojan (hence the Roman) nation (cf. *Aeneid* III, 104-105). The world has already passed through the ages of gold, silver, and bronze. The iron and clay feet probably signify the secular and spiritual authority on which "stood" the world of Dante's time.

105] In the golden age humanity knew no grief.

128-29] I. e. the river of blood (Canto XII), Phlegethon.

130] *Elsewhere*: on the summit of Purgatory (see *Purgatory* XXVIII, 125-29).

CANTO XV

2] Two towns indicating approximately the limits of the seacoast of mediaeval Flanders.

4] *Brenta*: river in the region of Padua.

6] *Chiarentana*: an ancient Duchy (Carinthia). The melted snow of its hills swells the Brenta and made necessary the erection of the dikes mentioned here.

27] *Brunetto Latini* (1210?-95): a Florentine Guelph at one time chancellor of the commune. Known for his books, the *Livre dou Tresor* and *Tesoretto*, a didactic allegory. Dante knew both these works and the *Comedy* shows their influence, particularly that of the *Tesoretto*. This would explain Dante's regarding him as a teacher; no doubt he received advice from him as well. There is no mention of his sin before Dante's allusion to it here. A. Pézard (*Dante sous la pluie de feu* [Paris: 1950]) argues that Brunetto's "perversion" consisted in his use of French rather than Tuscan for his great works.

60] *Fiésole*: a town occupying a hill some three miles from Florence. It was here, according to tradition, that Catiline's army was besieged by Caesar and compelled to surrender. It was then that the new city, Florence, was founded, the first inhabitants being Fiesolans, with the addition of some Roman soldiers (Villani, I, 38).

106] *Priscian*: this may be the grammarian of the sixth century (possibly confused with the fourth century heretical bishop Priscillian) or the professor of Bologna in the thirteenth century.

107] *Francis of Accorso*: celebrated professor of law at Bologna and Oxford in the second half of the thirteenth century.

109] *him*: Andrea dei Mozzi, Bishop of Florence from 1287 to 1295 when he was transferred to Vicenza (on the Bacchiglione), by Boniface VIII; the Popes spoke of themselves as the servants of God's servants; in view of Boniface's temperament there may be some irony in the phrase here.

122] The *pallium* is a banner given as a prize in a race run usually under municipal and ecclesiastical sponsorship. At Verona the green pallium was the prize for the foot race.

CANTO XVI

40] *Guido Guerra*: of the Conti Guidi, Guelph leader, fought for Charles at Benevento (died 1272). His grandmother, *Gualdrada*, was a daughter of the Bellincion Berti of *Paradise* xv, 112.

43] *Tegghiaio Aldobrandi*: of the Adimari clan (died 1267); he attempted to dissuade the Florentines from the campaign that ended with their defeat at Montaperti; line 44 seems to allude to this.

46] *Jácopo Rusticucci* (died sometime after 1266): was probably of humble origin, although the *Ottimo Commento* states that he was related to the Cavalcanti; he became a prominent and respected citizen. Benvenuto says he turned to vice because his wife was impossible to live with; this is an obvious gloss on an otherwise obscure reference.

72] *Guglielmo Borsiere*: "William the Pursemaker," who, according to Boccaccio, gave up his trade to become an "*uomo di corte*," i. e. an entertainer and sometimes a companion of the titled gentry. He appears in *Decameron* I, 8.

95 ff.] The fall of the Phlegethon is compared to that of the Montone, the first river between Monte Veso and the east that flows directly into the sea ("follows its own course") at the point called San Benedetto dell'Alpe. Before the confluence with other streams at Forlì, the Montone is called the Acquacheta. Sapegno reminds us that today the "first" stream would be the Reno, which was a tributary in Dante's day but now has its own outlet into the sea, and that it is in the course of the Acquacheta that the waterfall here referred to is to be found.

100-101] "The river roars because it falls over a single ledge, when it ought to be caught by a thousand. In dry weather the water trickles over a long series of steps at the side; when the stream is full it pours straight down the centre." (Grandgent, following Torraca.) Others interpret the passage to mean that the monastery of San Benedetto should have room for a thousand monks instead of the few in residence, still others see in it an allusion to a large castle fortress which the Conti Guidi were thinking of erecting on that spot. I have translated the passage with the first meaning in mind.

105] The symbolism of the cord is obscure. Some take it to mean that Dante had been a Franciscan, but this is not generally accepted nor does it explain the hidden meaning. Other suggestions include "continence" (Scartazzini), "the Law" (Momigliano) and "something to do with chastity" (Dorothy Sayers).

CANTO XVII

1] *the monster*: Geryon, a figure of classical mythology, a "three-bodied" monster (*Aeneid* vi, 289); Boccaccio describes him as a king of the Balearics luring with his blandishments unsuspecting travelers into his house and then murdering them. (*Genealogiae deorum* I, 21). It is Dante who gives him the unusual body here described.

18] Oriental rugs were already famous in the West.

19] *Arachne*: so skilled in weaving that the legend relates that she challenged Minerva and was changed into a spider for her presumption (*Met.* VI). See also *Purgatory* XII, 43-45.

23] It was believed that the beaver caught fish with his tail, sitting on the riverbanks with his forequarters out of the water, an "ambiguous posture," notes Sapegno, that points up the nature of Fraud.

56-57] The arms of the Gianfigliazzi of Florence; this is Catello di Rosso, of that clan.

58] Shield of the Obriachi, also Florentines; this is Ciapo.

59] *one*: this is Rinaldo degli Scrovegni of Padua; apparently only one of a number of usurers that this noble family produced. Some commentators in fact believe that Dante here describes the arms rather than the individual not only to indicate contempt by anonymity (as in Canto VII), but also to imply that these families were famous for their attachment to money.

63] According to the early commentators this would be Vitaliano de' Denti; since elsewhere he is mentioned as having a good character, Chimenz suggests that one Vitaliano di Jacopo Vitaliani, another Paduan, may be alluded to here.

67] The "sovereign" of all the usurers is Giovanni di Buiamonte, Florentine banker, knighted in 1298, later obliged to flee for embezzlement of funds. Died 1310. Rinaldo anticipates his eventual destiny just as Francesca had anticipated that of Gianciotto (Canto V). This device (somewhat unorthodox in its implications) enables Dante to pronounce his – if not necessarily God's – verdict on those who otherwise, in view of the date of the vision, might have escaped it.

74] Just how Reason has persuaded Fraud to its service we are not told. It is apparent from lines 40-41 that something more than the mere formula given Charon and Minos is necessary.

102] *Phaethon*: son of Apollo, who attempted to drive the chariot of the Sun. His inability to manage the horses would have led to the destruction of the earth had Jove not slain him with a thunderbolt (see *Met.* II).

104] *Icarus*: given wings by his father Daedalus, he flew too high; the sun's rays melted the wax which held the wings attached to his body and he fell into the sea (*Met.* VIII).

CANTO XVIII

23] In 1300 a year of jubilee was proclaimed by the Pope and many pilgrims came to Rome. Traffic across the St. Angelo Bridge which leads to the Vatican was routed as Dante describes. The castle (line 26) is the Castel St. Angelo, the mount (line 28) is Monte Giordano, or possibly the Capitoline, both on the bank opposite St. Peter's.

44] Venedico *Caccianemico*: Bolognese Guelph. The *marchese* of line 50, the seducer of Caccianemico's sister, the "fair Ghísola," is probably Opizzo II d'Este.

54] *'sipa'*: Bolognese dialect for *sì*, "yes."

55] *Sávena* and *Reno*: two rivers near Bologna.

78] *Jason*: winner of the Golden Fleece and seducer of Hypsipyle and Medea.

84] The women of Lemnos put all their men to death; Hypsipyle managed to save her father by guile, thus "betraying" the pact made by the women.

88] *Medea*: helped Jason to win the Fleece; he married her and subsequently abandoned her.

112] *Alessio* degli Interminei: member of a noble family of Lucca.

122] *Thaïs*: the harlot of Terence's *Eunuchus*. Like Pope Anastasius (Canto XI) she is in Hell by mistake, for it was not she, but the parasite Gnatho who uttered the response here cited as typical of the flatterer. Dante had not read Terence but was following the account given in Cicero's *De Amicitia* XXVI; unfamiliar with the context of the play, he attributed the remark to Thaïs rather than Gnatho.

CANTO XIX

1] *Simon Magus* (Acts 8: 9-24) was chided by St. Peter for thinking God's gifts could be purchased with money.

18] Around the baptismal font of the Baptistry of Florence niches were carved out for the assisting priests. Apparently Dante broke through one of these to save a child in the font and his enemies chose to regard his act as sacrilegious. We have only his own account of this incident.

49] Convicted assassins were buried alive, bound head down to a stake. It may well be understood how the criminal, in such a state, might summon his confessor repeatedly to postpone the time when the earth would be thrown in to suffocate him.

51] *Boniface* VIII: Pope from 1294 to 1303 and Dante's arch-enemy. This scene illustrates Dante's ingenuity in indicating the fate of those still living at the time of the ideal date of the vision. See Cantos V and XVII.

56] *The fairest lady*: the Church.

67-68] Nicholas III, Pope from 1277 to 1280. Nicholas was of the Orsini family and *orsa* is "she-bear" in Italian.

80-82] *another*: Clement V, Pope from 1305 to 1314. He was regarded as a tool of Philip the Fair of France and moved the Papal See from Rome to Avignon. Before assuming the tiara he was Archbishop of Bordeaux; hence he came "from out the west."

83] Jason bribed Antiochus Epiphanes to name him high priest (II Mac. 4: 7 ff.).

89-90] See Matthew 4: 19; John 21: 19.

93-94] See Acts 1: 13-26; *the guilty soul*: Judas.

97] Nicholas opposed Charles of Anjou who lost Sicily in the uprising known as "the Sicilian Vespers." The "ill-gotten gains" have been interpreted as referring to tithes misused for political purposes or to bribes taken from the Eastern Emperor, also an enemy of Charles.

105-108] Revelations 17 speaks of "the great whore that sitteth upon the waters." Dante took the figure as a symbol of the corrupt Church. The heads and horns in the vision of the Evangelist are attributed to the beast on which the "whore" is riding; Dante assigns them instead to the woman. They symbolize respectively the seven gifts of the Holy Spirit (or the seven sacraments) and the ten commandments. The *"spouse"* of line 108 is the papacy.

112] The Emperor Constantine was believed to have made a gift of the Western Empire to Pope Sylvester. This "donation" was proved in the Renaissance to be without historical foundation. Dante accepted it as true, but deplored it. (I have borrowed Milton's version of 112-14, translated in his *Reformation in England*, 1641).

CANTO XX

34] *Amphiaraus*: one of the seven besiegers of Thebes. Statius (*Thebaid*) tells of the earth opening beneath his feet in the midst of battle.

40] *Tiresias*: soothsayer of Thebes. The story of his change of sex is told in *Metamorphoses* III.

45] *Aruns*: the Etruscan prophesied the civil war between Caesar and Pompey (*Pharsalia* I, 584-638).

52] *Manto*: daughter of Tiresias.

57] After the death of Eteocles and Polynices, Thebes was ruled by the tyrant Creon.

65] Probably the little island now known as Lechi in Lake Garda (Chimenz).

93-94] Alberto di Casalodi, on the treacherous advice of Pinamonte Bonaccorsi, exiled many of the nobles. Pinamonte then took advantage of the situation to make himself master of the town, banishing Alberto and killing many of his leading citizens (Benvenuto).

95-96] These lines suggest the reason for this somewhat puzzling excursus. In the *Aeneid* Virgil had said that Mantua had been founded by Ocnus, the son of Manto. Since Dante believes otherwise he courteously allows Virgil to make the correction himself. Various commentators have remarked that the insistence that Manto did not actually found the city and that the name was chosen without appeal to augury combine to indicate Virgil's desire to detach himself from any relation with sorcery or occult practices. Or, in other terms, Dante is making the point that Virgil is no sorcerer, even though such was his fame in the middle ages.

110] *Euripilus*: appears in *Aeneid* II, 113 ff. where there is no reference to his office in Aulis. Possibly Dante's version of the *Aeneid* was so phrased as to lead him to make this assumption (Chimenz, following Parodi).

114] *Michael Scot*: celebrated mediaeval philosopher, alchemist and scholar (1214?-91), for several years at the court of Frederick II. His fame as a wizard is posthumous, the popes Honorius III and Gregory IX thought highly of him (Toynbee). No one knows why Dante thought of him as "slender in the flanks."

116] *Guido Bonatti*: celebrated astrologer of the thirteenth century, for some time at the court of Frederick II.
Asdente: a shoemaker of Parma who had the reputation of a prophet; Dante mentions him in *Convivio* IV, XVI, 50-71.

271

122] *Cain with his thorns*: "The man in the moon" was seen as Cain with his burden of thorns. The passage means that the moon, one night past full, is now directly over the line which divides the hemisphere of land from that of water. From the point of view of an observer in Jerusalem, Virgil's point of reckoning, the moon is setting over Seville. Since at no point was it of disservice to Dante during his lost night (i. e. since it was of constant advantage to him), its hour of setting is after sunrise. In short it is now about six o'clock Saturday morning.

CANTO XXI

36] *Saint Zita*: patron saint of Lucca.

39] *Bonturo* (Dati): not simply a barrator but an "arch-barrator" (Benvenuto). Dante is ironical here.

46] *The Holy Face*: a wooden image of Christ, venerated in Lucca.

48] *Serchio*: a river near Lucca.

91] *Caprona*: fortress near Pisa taken by the Guelphs in 1289. Apparently Dante was a member of the besieging forces.

106-108] Another allusion to the earthquake that followed the Crucifixion. Dante, following Luke, held that the death on the Cross took place at noon. (*Convivio* IV, XXIII, 10-11). It is 7:00 A.M. as Malacoda speaks.

111] On the proper names in this passage Grandgent comments: "Their generic designation is *Malebranche*, 'Badpaws'; *Alichino* is perhaps the French *Harlequin*, leader of the Wild Hunt; *Farfarello* seems to be a traditional demon name; *Barbariccia*, *Cagnazzo*, *Graffiacane*, *Malacoda*, *Rubicante* mean respectively 'Curlybeard,' 'Mean Dog,' 'Dogscratcher,' 'Badtail,' 'Rubicund.' Some of the appellations appear to be ludicrous distortions of the names of real people: there was a prominent Malabranca family in Rome; the Raffacani were numerous in Florence; a Pietro di Malacoda is attested; and Torraca cites among others, Canasso, Scaldabrina, Ciriolo, Dragonetto, Biccicocco, Scormiglio . . ."

CANTO XXII

5] Dante took part in the battle of Campaldino (1289) fought near Arezzo.

21] Dolphins were believed to give sailors warning of storms.

49] The speaker has been identified as one Ciampolo, though nothing more is known of him than what Dante tells us.

52] Thibault II (1253-1270).

79] *Gallura*: one of the four districts into which the Pisans divided Sardinia. Logodoro (line 87) is another. Nothing certain can be added to what Dante tells of Brother Gomita and Michael Zanche.

CANTO XXIII

5] The story Dante has reference to tells of a frog ferrying a mouse across a river. The frog treacherously attempting to drown the mouse is, in its turn, attacked by a hawk; the mouse escapes. The fable is not Aesop's but was attributed to him.

60] *Cluny*: celebrated Benedictine monastery in east central France. Some commentators believe the monks of Cologne in Germany are here referred to.

63] Frederick II, to quote one of the older commentators, punished those guilty of *lèse majesté* by having them wrapped in leaden cloaks and thrown into a heated cauldron. There is no historical evidence for this tale, but Dante evidently believed it.

99] The brothers of the lay order of Beata Maria were known as Frati Godenti (Merry Friars), for they were not bound by the usual stringent vows.

100-104] Catalano de' Catalani, a Guelph, and Loderingo degli Andalò, a Ghibelline: in the Middle Ages Italian towns, rent as they were by factions, frequently chose their chief magistrate, called the *podestà*, from some other city. The two friars were made joint *podestà* of Florence in 1266. They were unsuccessful in keeping the peace and in the course of civil strife the Gardingo quarter was ravaged.

113] Caiaphas, the High Priest. See John 11: 49-50.

118] Annas, the father-in-law of Caiaphas. See John 18: 13, 14, 24.

121] Virgil's previous descent took place before the Crucifixion.

136] I. e., from Badtail.

138] Reference is to the University, oldest in Italy and famous for law.

CANTO XXIV

6] *her sister*: snow.

57] An allusion to the Mount of Purgatory which Dante must climb to meet Beatrice.

90] *cenchres, amphisbenes*: fabulous serpents mentioned by Lucan, *Pharsalia* IX, 700 ff.

98] *heliotrope*: a magic stone that would render its wearer invisible; cf. *Decameron* VIII, 3.

111] This mythological bird, dear to the Middle Ages, was described by Ovid (*Met.* XV, 392 ff.). Dante may have encountered it in the pages of Pliny or Brunetto Latini.

129] *Vanni Fucci*: a natural son of one of the Lazzari family of Pistoia and a well-known robber.

133] Dante would have expected to find him among the violent in the first ring of the seventh circle.

142] The sacristy of the Cathedral of Pistoia.

147 ff.] The Black Guelphs were driven from Pistoia in May of 1301. In November of the same year under the protection of Charles of Valois certain powerful Black families returned to Florence and drove out the Whites. Subsequently Moroello Malaspina (the "bolt") moved from Val di Magra to attack the Whites of Pistoia. Though at first surrounded by the enemy ("enveloped in thick clouds"), he de-

feated them at Serravalle (which Dante calls Campo Piceno). There are other interpretations of this somewhat obscure prophecy.

CANTO XXV

2] A gesture made by inserting the thumb between the first and second fingers. An obscene and insulting sign in Latin countries.

12] Pistoia was supposed to have been founded by the remnants of Catiline's army.

15] *him*: Capaneus; see Canto XIV, line 49, note.

19] *Maremma*: see note to Canto XIII, line 7.

25] *Cacus*: legendary monster slain by Hercules; see *Aeneid* VIII, 194, where he is described as "half-man." Dante made him a centaur.

28] *above*: in the first ring of the violent; see Canto XII.

42] *Cianfa*: identified as one of the Donati of Florence (Toynbee).

66] *Agnel* Brunelleschi: a thief from childhood, according to the *Anonimo fiorentino*.

85] The umbilicus.

93 ff.] Lucan (*Pharsalia* IX) tells of the strange effects of snake bites; Sabellus when bitten melts away like snow, Nisidius swells up and bursts his armor. The transformations of Cadmus and Arethusa are described in Ovid's *Metamorphoses* (IV and V respectively).

136] It was believed that human saliva was poisonous to snakes.

139] Variously identified as Buoso de' Donati or Buoso degli Abati, both of Florence.

146] *Puccio* de Galigai: a Florentine Ghibelline.

148] *the third*: Guercio de' Cavalcanti. The people of Gaville (a village on the Arno) killed him and his kinsmen took revenge on the village.

CANTO XXVI

9] *Prato*: small city a few miles north of Florence. Prato rebelled and drove out the Blacks in 1309. The reference, however, may be more general, meaning simply that all Florence's neighbors wish her ill. Some see an allusion to the Cardinal da Prato and the interdiction laid on Florence by him in 1304.

34 ff.] Elijah was carried off to Heaven in a chariot of fire. Elisha, who had witnessed his ascent, was mocked by children; in punishment for this bears came forth and devoured them (II Kings 2: 11, 12, 23, 24).

56] *The Theban brothers*: Eteocles and Polynices, rivals for the succession to the throne of ancient Thebes. They slew each other and so bitter was their hatred that the fire rising from their funeral pyre was split into two flames (*Thebaid* XII, 420 ff.).

57-58] *Diomed*; *Ulysses*: heroes of the *Iliad*.

61-63] The Trojan Horse.

65] Achilles was sought out in hiding by Diomed and Ulysses who persuaded him to leave Deidamía who had borne him a son. Deidamía died of grief.

67] The Palladium was a statue of Pallas revered in Troy. The fate of the city was said to depend on its safekeeping: Ulysses succeeded in stealing it.

95] *Gaeta*: on Tyrrhenian Sea between Naples and Rome. It was named by Aeneas after his old nurse (*Aeneid* VII, 1-4).

112] The ancients commonly regarded the pillars of Hercules (that is, Gibraltar and Mount Abyla on the African shore) as the limits of the world of men.

114] *Ceuta*: in Morocco.

127-29] Ulysses' course is to the southeast – the same taken by the Genoese Vivaldi brothers in 1291 – and later by Columbus.

136] "The Christian listener . . . cannot for an instant doubt that the lofty dusky mountain . . . is the Purgatorial mount" (Vossler).

144] *One*: God, seldom named in the *Inferno*.

CANTO XXVII

7] Perillus of Athens, so the story goes, invented a bronze bull, hollow within. Offenders against the tyrant Phalaris of Sicily, whom the inventor served, were placed inside and, when the "bull" was heated, gradually roasted. Their screams of pain gave the effect of the bull's roaring. This ingenious device was tested first on its inventor. The story goes back to Ovid; Dante may have found it in Orosius.

20] *Istra* is a Lombard word meaning "now"; if we adopt that reading then Virgil has been speaking in dialect. Some texts have *issa*; this is a Tuscan word and we should assume, with that reading, that Virgil simply had a Lombard accent. But in any case why he should reveal this provincialism for the only time in the poem while speaking to a classical figure is hard to say. For Momigliano (and others) this is a *stonatura*.

28] *Romagnoli*: the inhabitants of Romagna, a region in Northeastern Italy, including such towns as Ravenna, Rimini, Faenza, and Imola. The speaker is Guido da Montefeltro (1220?-98), Ghibelline soldier and politician of whom Dante elsewhere (*Convivio* IV, XXVIII, 8-9) speaks with respect.

29-30] Between Urbino and Monte Coronaro "whence the Tiber springs" is the area known as Montefeltro, also a part of Romagna.

41] *Polenta*: Lords of Ravenna, see Canto V, line 71, note; an eagle formed part of their crest.

42] *Cervia*: small town on the Adriatic, near Ravenna.
The city: Forlì, a Ghibelline center. In 1282 Guido da Montefeltro made a successful sortie from the town, under siege by the French troops fighting for the Guelphs; many of the besiegers were slain. In 1300 Forlì was in the hands of the Ordelaffi, whose arms bore a lion with green forequarters.

46] The old mastiff is Malatesta da Verrucchio, Lord of Rimini, father of Paolo and Gianciotto; the young mastiff is Malatestino, yet another son.

47] *Montagna*: the Ghibelline leader, Montagna de' Parcitati, treacherously taken prisoner by the old mastiff and murdered (1295) by the young one (Toynbee).

275

49-51] Faenza on the Lamone and Imola near the Santerno were under the despot Maghinardo di Pagano da Susinana; his shield was a blue lion on a white field. He was noted for his frequent changes of allegiance from Guelph to Ghibelline and vice versa.

52] This is Cesena which "preserved the forms of municipal self-government, but was ruled, from 1296 to 1300, by a boss, Galasso da Montefeltro, a cousin of Guido" (Grandgent).

56] I. e., I've answered your question, please now answer mine.

67] Guido became a Franciscan in his old age.

70] *the High Priest*: Boniface VIII (see Canto XIX, line 51). Boniface was waging war against the Colonna family who had retired to the fortress of Palestrina.

88] Acre, which had been in the possession of the Christians for a hundred years, had been retaken by the Saracens in 1291.

89] In spite of the prohibition of the Church, many Christians carried on trade with Saracens.

93] *Soracte*: the Emperor Constantine, stricken with leprosy, sought aid from Pope Sylvester, living in a cave under Mount Soracte. The successful healing resulted in the Emperor's conversion and in the Donation of Constantine (see Canto XIX, line 112). All this was accepted as fact in the Middle Ages.

106] *predecessor*: Celestinus V (see Canto III, line 59, note).

CANTO XXVIII

10-11] The first wars here referred to are those between the Romans (the descendants of the Trojans) and the Samnites (343-290 B.C.). The "later strife" is the struggle between Rome and Carthage (264-146 B.C.) with particular reference to the battle of Cannae (216 B.C.) at which the slaughter of the Romans was so great that baskets of gold rings taken from the slain were brought to the Carthaginian Senate.

16] *Robert Guiscard*: the Norman, fought numerous engagements against Greeks and Saracens in Southern Italy in the latter part of the eleventh century.

18] *Ceperano*: the defection of the barons of Apulia, detached to hold the pass of Ceperano on the Liri River, helped bring about the defeat of Manfred, Ghibelline leader, at Benevento (1266).

19] *Tagliacozzo*: site of the crucial battle between Conradin, nephew of Manfred, and Charles of Anjou. The latter was victorious through a stratagem suggested by Erard (Alardo) de Valery (1268).

35] *Mahomet* (570-632): in Dante's view the greatest of all schismatics. Ali was his son-in-law and successor in the Caliphate.

58] *Fra Dolcino* (Tornielli): leader of the sect known as the Apostolic Brothers, accused of practicing communism of goods and women. Clement V proclaimed a crusade against the brotherhood which, in 1306, found itself surrounded by a large attacking force, largely made up of Novarese (Novara is a city of Northern Piedmont), and being cut off by heavy snows from any opportunity of getting supplies, obliged to surrender. Dolcino was burnt at Vercelli (1307).

73] *Medicina*: a town near Bologna. Pier, according to the ancient commentators, stirred up dissension among the lords of Romagna.

75] *Vercelli*: in Piedmont; *Marcabò*: a castle near Ravenna. The plain is the Po Valley, taking in a large part of Romagna.

76 ff.] Malatestino, the one-eyed tyrant of Rimini, hoping to annex Fano (a small town on the Adriatic south of Rimini), lured the two principal citizens, Angiolello da Carignano and Guido del Cassero, to a parley at Cattólica, a cape between the two towns. There he succeeded by treachery in having them drowned. Focara, a promontory between Fano and Cattólica, was notorious for its strong winds, but inasmuch as the two victims did not live to reach the point they had no need to offer the usual prayers and vows. Dante himself is our best authority for the whole story.

82-84] That is, never was such a dastardly crime committed throughout the whole Mediterranean, not even by pirates or by the (proverbially treacherous) Greeks.

97] According to Lucan, Curio urged Caesar to cross the Rubicon and attack the republic (*Pharsalia* I, 280 ff.). Curio had been exiled from Rome when he gave this advice.

106] *Mosca*: dei Lamberti. When one of the Bondelmonti offended the Amidei family it was suggested that he be beaten. Mosca proposed that he be killed and have the thing done with. His advice was accepted and, the Bondelmonti being aroused, a feud began which involved most of the families of Tuscany and soon came to have political coloration, for Guelph and Ghibelline took opposite sides. The Lamberti, Ghibellines, were banished from Florence in 1258, hence Dante's remark in line 110.

135] *Bertran de Born* (1140?-1215): a celebrated Provençal troubadour and warrior-politician. He was believed to have created dissension between Henry II of England and his son, called the "young king," for he was crowned during his father's lifetime though he never lived to reign. Bertran's lament for the young king has been translated by Ezra Pound.

132-39] See II Samuel 15-17.

CANTO XXIX

25] *Geri*: a distant kinsman of Dante, slain in a feud. Dante seems to feel some obligation to avenge him.

26] *Hautefort*: Bertran de Born's castle.

44] *Valdichiana*: near Arezzo; in Dante's time an unhealthy region, as were the Maremma (Canto XIII, line 7, note) and Sardinia.

58] Juno, in her jealous rage against the nymph Aegina, who had borne Jove a son, sent a plague which consumed all men and animals on the island, also called Aegina, where the nymph lived. The sole survivor was the son, Aeacus, who prayed to Jove to change the ants into men. Jove answered the prayer. (*Met.* VII, 523-657.)

106 ff.] The speaker is Maestro Griffolino; little is known of him save what he tells us; Albero seems to have been a wealthy Sienese.

117-18] Dante voices a common Florentine opinion.

120] *the other*: Capocchio, burned in Siena in 1293.

121-28] The passage is ironic; Capocchio is citing the outstanding examples of Sienese dissipation. Stricca is probably Giovanni Stricca de' Salimbeni; Niccolò, his brother, gets credit for introducing the use of cloves as a spice into the Sienese cuisine ("that garden" is Siena). Caccia has been identified as the poet Caccia da Siena. He was a member of the "spendthrift brigade" of young Sienese wastrels. Abbagliato (a nickname translated "muddlehead" by Toynbee) refers to one Meo Folcacchieri, who held high offices in Siena (chancellor in 1279). It is not certain whether the reference to his wit is ironic or whether he endeavored in vain to suppress the "brigade."

CANTO XXX

1 ff.] The story of the madness of Athamas is told in *Metamorphoses* IV, that of Hecuba in *Metamorphoses* XIII. For Polyxena and Polydorus, Canto V, line 63, note, and Canto XIII, line 45, note, respectively.

28] *The Aretine*: Griffolino.

35] The story of the incestuous Myrrha is in *Metamorphoses* X.

38] *he*: Gianni Schicchi. It is related that he took the place of the dying Buoso Donati and made a will to satisfy the anxious heir. Incidentally, he willed to himself Donati's highly prized mare, "the lady of the troop."

61] *Casentino*: the region of upper Arno.

69] *Romena*: castle of the Conti Guidi, mentioned in line 73. The florin (coin of Florence) was stamped with the image of John the Baptist.

74] *Branda's spring*: near Romena.

93] *the soul*: Potiphar's wife (see Gen. 39: 6-20).

94] Sinon, pretending to be on their side, persuaded the Trojans to take in the wooden horse (*Aeneid* II, 57 ff.).

124] *Narcissus' glass*: water.

CANTO XXXI

3] A reference to this magic lance is found in *Metamorphoses* XXIII, 171.

15] The blast blown by Roland to summon Charlemagne to his aid was heard for thirty leagues, according to the *Chanson de Roland*.

40] Twelve towers crowned the walls of Montereggione in Valdelsa, built in 1213 by the Sienese.

43] Jove dealt his bolts against the Titans at Phlegra (see Canto XIV, line 56, note). The ancients believed that by thunder he still indicated his displeasure with them.

58] A huge pine cone of bronze which is now in the Belvedere garden of the Vatican. In Dante's time it stood in front of St. Peter's.

63] The Frisians were famous for their great stature.

66] See line 80.

76] *Nimrod*: first king of Babylon; he it was who planned the tower of Babel (Gen. 10: 8-10). In the Bible he is merely a "mighty hunter" but Orosius and St. Augustine (*Civ. Dei* XVI, 3, 4, 11) make him a giant.

90] *Ephialtes*: son of Neptune, one of the most bellicose of the Titans.

96] *Briareus*: son of Uranus and Earth.

97] *Antaeus*: son of Neptune and Earth. Hercules wrestled with him and could conquer him only by holding him above the Earth whence he drew his strength.

111] The African valley which was the habitat of Antaeus was also the scene of Scipio's triumph over Hannibal at Zama.

114] According to Lucan (*Pharsalia* IV, 590).

118] Antaeus was not born at the time of Phlegra.

121] *Tityos* and *Typhon*: two other giants.

133] *Garisenda*: a leaning tower in Bologna. If one stands under the leaning side and looks up and sees a cloud floating in the direction opposite the slant the tower does in fact seem to be falling.

CANTO XXXII

10] Amphion's lyre, inspired by the Muses, caused rocks to rise and form the walls of Thebes (see *Thebaid* X, 873 ff.).

28-29] *Tambernic*: probably a mountain in Slavonia, though identification is uncertain. *Pietrapiana*: a peak in the Apennines.

56] *Bisenzo*: a small stream near Prato; in the vicinity of Mangona, the home of Albert. The two sons killed each other in a quarrel over their inheritance (Benvenuto).

61] *the traitorous soul*: Mordred, the traitorous knight of the Round Table. Arthur dealt him such a wound that, the tale tells, sunlight poured through the hole in his body (see Toynbee under Artù).

63] *Foccaccia*: de' Cancellieri of Pistoia, slayer of one of his kinsmen.

65] *Sassol Mascheroni*: murderer of a youthful cousin.

67] *Camición dei Pazzi*: another slayer of a youthful relative, according to the ancient commentators. Carlino, his brother, betrayed the White Party, surrendering a fortress to the Blacks. He died in 1302; hence he is still awaited in Hell in 1300.

80] *Montaperti*: see Canto X. It is the mention of this name that causes Dante to interrogate further the unhappy soul.

88] *Antenora*: second division of the ninth circle in which are punished traitors to country and party. So called after Antenor, the Trojan, who according to a mediaeval legend, betrayed his fatherland.

105] *Bocca* (degli Abati): Florentine Guelph, whose treachery was instrumental in the defeat of his party at Montaperti (Villani, VI, 78).

116] Buoso da Duera, bribed by the French to betray the Ghibellines under Manfred (Villani, VII, 4).

119] Tesauro dei *Beccherìa*: papal legate in Tuscany. He was charged with conspiring with the Ghibelline exiles and decapitated (1268). Villani, VI, 65 seems to think he was innocent.

121] *Gian de' Soldanieri*: Florentine Ghibelline traitor (Villani, VII, 14).

122] *Ganelon*: the treacherous knight in the *Chanson de Roland*.
Tebaldello degli Zambrasi: treacherously surrendered his own city of Faenza to the Guelphs. Salimbene gives details.

130] *Tydeus*: one of the Seven against Thebes, was mortally wounded in combat with Menalippus. He succeeded in killing his adversary, however, and before dying had the head of his enemy brought to him and gnawed it in his rage (*Thebaid* VIII).

CANTO XXXIII

13-14] *Count Ugolino* della Gherardesca: leader of one faction of the Pisan Guelphs. In 1288 he betrayed his own party by plotting with the Archbishop Ruggieri, the head of the Ghibellines. In turn he was betrayed by the Archbishop, who caused the imprisonment and death of the Count and four of his children and grandchildren in the manner described in this canto. (See Villani, VII, 121, 128.)

28] *the hill*: Monte San Giuliano, between Lucca and Pisa.

31] Ghibelline families of Pisa.

74] Most commentators interpret this line to mean that Ugolino died, not that he resorted to cannibalism.

81] Islands off the Tuscan coast, under the rule of Pisa.

85] In 1284, after the Pisans had been defeated by the Genoese, Ugolino had surrendered some fortified castles to Florence and Lucca. This may have been a necessary measure but was considered treason by many.

88] Ancient Thebes was notorious for the cruelty and savagery of its civil strife. Uguccione and Brigata are names of the children of Ugolino.

115] *Fra Alberigo*: another of the "jovial Friars" (see Canto XXIII, note to line 99), murdered his brother and his nephews at a banquet he offered them in Faenza (1285). The signal for the killing was the phrase "Bring in the fruit," and "The bad fruit of Fra Alberigo" became a proverbial expression. The affair is alluded to by Villani (x, 27) and details are given by Benvenuto.

121] *Ptolomaea*: so called, it would seem, from the Ptolemy of I Maccabees (16: 11-17) who treacherously murdered three guests.

123] *Atropos*: one of the Fates.

134] *Branca d'Oria*: of Genoa, murderer of his father-in-law Michael Zanche (see below, line 139 and also Canto XXII, line 86), whom he had invited to a banquet. Branca was aided by a nephew, referred to in line 143.

1] "The banners of Hell's King come forth," a slightly altered version of the sixth-century hymn of Fortunatus.

36] The colors of the three faces symbolize hatred, impotence, and ignorance, the opposite of love, power, and wisdom, which are attributes of the Trinity, such is the interpretation of most of the old commentators; Scartazzini's gloss summarizes the other and less likely ones.

93] *tierce*: the first three hours of the morning.

108] I. e., the center of the earth.

118] It was believed that when Lucifer fell, all the land of the hemisphere where he struck moved away and left a void which was filled up by the sea. Dante hazards the hypothesis that the land which once filled the other side of Judecca and through which Satan must once have passed, rose on the watery hemisphere to form the mount of Purgatory.

133] Compare Canto IV, 15.

136] It is just before dawn on Easter Sunday.